TURNING OF THE TIDE

Jaytoe Anthony Tukan, Sr.
Kalawantis Publishing Services, Inc.
www.kalawantis.com
author@kalawantis.com

Dedication

Niecy and our beautiful children, I could not ask God for a more wonderful family. I am grateful to our Father.

ISBN: 13:978-1542922630
ISBN: 10:1542922631

ACKNOWLEDGMENTS

Writing and publishing a book is a great responsibility which many authors do not ever underestimate. Yet, along with this important duty, come many uncalled-for sacrifices endured by family members, especially the children, some of whom may not truly understand while daddy spends so much time at the computer, time he could have spent with the family. It is with this understanding that I extend my sincere thanks and appreciation to you, children, and to your mom, for your patience, and your many ideas expressed, which became a great contribution to this writing. I love you all.

"The stone which the builders rejected, has become the Chief Cornerstone."

Matthew 21: 42

Some leaders are born, while others are made. Where do you place President Obama? Is he a born or made leader?

Table of Contents

Table of Contents

Introduction

Jaytoe Anthony Tukan gives us a different look at the life of President Obama. The author answers two important questions: why did Barack's father turn down a scholarship offer (1962) from New York University with sufficient money to keep his family together, but decided, instead to do his graduate study at Harvard University? Why did he return to Africa without taking baby Barack and his mother with him? In answering these questions, Jaytoe presents a different perspective on the life of the President's father.

While one may think that this book is only about politics, it is nonetheless, mostly about culture, tradition, family, dreams, and inspirations. It presents two families from two different continents, separated by the great Atlantic Ocean, yet so close that distance, religion, ethnicity, nationality, or political ideologies, could not prevent them from forming a unified family tie.

The interviews conducted with the general public are found in two chapters: America Speaks and Universal Health Insurance. Read citizens opinions why Mr. Obama won the U.S. Presidency that Rev. Jesse Jackson or Rev. Al Sharpton did not win when they ran. Is there a major difference between Obama and the other black people who ran before him? Secondly, you will also see what

TURNING OF THE TIDE

Americans think about the President's Universal Health Insurance, or Obamacare.

Is the rejected stone now the Chief Cornerstone? President Obama was considered by some Americans as being weak and not able to fight terrorism. Yet the Obama Administration has eliminated from the world, Osama bin Laden, the world's Number One Terrorist. Do we now believe that the President can deal with and/or fight terrorism, the way some Americans never thought possible?

Chapter One

Rising Waves

HAS THE TIDE TURNED? The waves roar and continue raging! The fierce current gets stronger and stronger every second. He tries very, very hard to save himself, but the current sends him way up in the air, as if he's reaching for the sky, only to let him down again into the deep. The deep, perhaps the deepest of all waters, could not have been more unkind. As all look on, and all hearts beat for fear the black boy might drown, the current brings him way back up again. And everyone cheers, with relief that he will be saved.

Like a roaring lion, however, the waves roar again. Out of a sudden, it is quiet once more, and everyone becomes motionless again. Nobody knows what will happen next, or what to expect any more, as all hearts continue to beat intensely, the waves

TURNING OF THE TIDE

rage and rage. It seems there is no way out.

His friend, a white boy, when he does not see his black friend any more, tries to rush into the deep to save him. But he's held back. And the voices from some bystanders echo to the white boy: "No! Leave him be! Let him drown! Let him die!"

Again the black boy comes up, but this time, only his head is up - gasping for air once more. Then into the deep he sinks! The waves, and the current, all continue to roar and rise. Then the seconds tick and tick! Only this time, the seconds turn quickly into minutes, and the minutes, - hours, and this time will be his last. This is the last time all his friends and the rest of the bystanders will see him alive again.

He's gone! He has fallen victim to hate, to slavery and racism! But nothing is done at all! Nothing is done to avenge his death. No one would dare say a word, or put up a fight. What for? Was the tide ready to turn? No, there was no **turning of the tide!** At least not then and there.

Fight? What fight? What would be the point of the fight? Who would dare try to fight to turn the tide? Doing so would be suicidal. More and more black boys would be killed; more black girls would be raped! More Negroes would be arrested and very

Jaytoe Anthony Tukan, Sr.

TURNING OF THE TIDE

much humiliated right before the eyes of families and friends; they would be taken into police cells for no good reason. For what? For the color of their skin?

And so many years later, the young assistant pastor of the Ebenezer Baptist Church in Atlanta, Georgia, would say: "I have a dream that my four little children will one day live in a nation where they will not be judged by the color of their skin, but by the content of their character."

These familiar words from the Rev. Martin Luther King, Jr., could not have been more real and fulfilled in America today. A great country, yet a racially divided nation for more than two centuries, America has now decided to change course, a new path very necessary, indeed. It has been a long time coming, and a rough and narrow road for a nation to travel. Nevertheless, on Tuesday, November 4, 2008, the nation watched, together with the whole world, in anticipation and anxiety of what was about to go down in history as a **Turning of the tide in America.** It was time for the **tide** to let down, never to rise again, to a point of blockade that others might get through, or cross over to the other side. A great turning of the tide, indeed!

"A beacon light" shining atop a little hill, but

13   **Jaytoe Anthony Tukan, Sr.**

TURNING OF THE TIDE

still hidden for many, many years, was yet to be discovered. "A beacon light of hope," as Dr. King would say, in the midst of a despairing people, is now truly ready to brightening........up its disjointed surrounding, which shamefully so, happens to be our community, our society, and our nation. Indeed, it is this <u>one nation</u>, which we all love, cherish, and honor, as we pledge our: *'allegiance to the Flag of the United States of America, and to the Republic for which it stands, <u>one nation</u>, under God, indivisible, with liberty, and justice for all.'*

On this day, Tuesday, November 4, 2008, Barack Obama becomes the very first African American to be elected President of the United States of America. He is the 44th President of the country. The announcement was made on all the networks, while some of us saw such a unanimous vote coming to us from CNN at exactly 11:00 P.M., Eastern Time.

The dreamer might have been separated from this world, but has the **dream** departed with him? No, the dream is truly alive and well. Because the dream has survived and is alive, a black person is now the president of this country. I do believe Dr. King and his wife, Coretta, are in deed smiling and very well sharing tears of joy right at this moment,

Jaytoe Anthony Tukan, Sr.

TURNING OF THE TIDE

seeing what's happening in America today. They must be dropping tears of joy, similar to the teardrops which came down the cheeks of the Rev. Jesse Jackson, as we all watched our newly elected President, Barack Hussein Obama, deliver his acceptance speech. A dream never dies! The Dream, it lives on!

Would a person destined for greatness in life not have the drive to be great, even while still a child? Does it ever matter what obstacles stand in the way? Will the obstacles cause the person to give up so easily, and then wonder what could have been? I believe that a child who will be somebody, will have the determination from the very beginning, from the get-go, to be somebody, regardless how high the mountains are that he or she has to climb. If there are rugged areas over which to tread before getting to the top, these rough areas were only there to prepare the child for such a journey to greatness.

For many would-be great people, there will be those bumpy roads to travel, those rough valleys to live in, those deep swamps, or fierce currents of rivers to cross. At times, there will be, more than likely, torrential rains and violent storms; against all of these, that child must learn how to survive before moving onto the top. How can one ever get to the top, and most importantly, remain at the top, if such a person is not able to survive while still in the valley?

Isn't a purpose-driven life one that is full of dreams? Do we have any reason to honestly believe that a first grade student would really know how to differentiate dreams from fantasies? When he was in the first grade, it is said that Barack wrote a paper for his class assignment, which he titled: "I want to be President." Can you believe this? Did he actually believe he would be president of the United States someday? Or was he really talking about being president for his first grade class?

What about little William Jefferson Clinton, whose class was on a school trip to the White House? Shaking hands with President Kennedy, Clinton told the President that he, too, would grow up someday and be president. Was that a dream or fantasy? This story was told over and over about Clinton during his campaigning and presidency in the 1990s.

How do our childhood fantasies really turn into dreams? Fantasies they might have been, history does speak for itself about Obama and Clinton.

Do you have any fantasies? They can turn into dreams. It all depends on what part of the world you

TURNING OF THE TIDE

are, and who is in your corner. The mind-set must be focused. The environment must be right. And most importantly, your drive must be in tack. Dreaming is a necessary part of life. But life without dreams? Is it really life? Is it worth living? Do you have a dream? How is your purposed-driven life?

Each of us must find something about which to dream; dream to be somebody better. I think Henry Wadsworth Longfellow sums it up for us in his *Psalm of Life,* "But to act, that each tomorrow find us farther than today."

Each of us must strive to progress in life daily, regardless what the current situation may be. Even in the midst of economic uncertainty, or sometimes under a gloomy sky, we must rather not despair; we must continue to fight to foster every day, that our tomorrow be better than our today. Let each of us dream each night that we will work very diligently and sensibly each day for a better tomorrow. Let us dream to help a brother when we realize that he is traveling on the wrong path of life. Let us do our very best to encourage a sister to keep the faith, because there comes a brighter tomorrow only if she hangs in there a little while longer. Only if we patiently endure, there is that light at the 'other end of the tunnel.'

Jaytoe Anthony Tukan, Sr.

TURNING OF THE TIDE

Goal-setting is truly a necessary part of dreaming. Short-term or long-term goals, we must set them. Not only should we set goals, we must work very hard towards accomplishing each of them, being patient when there is an obstacle in achieving any goal. Patience is a virtue which must truly be exercised if we want to truly succeed.

Does it mean that all of my dreams will turn into realities? Probably not, but this should not stop me from dreaming. Dreaming, however, must come from within; it is not something another person tells me to do. Having said that, I might still add that there is nothing wrong with being inspired by another person. Maybe that could be all that I need; it may serve as a path-setter to help me find my way to something about which to dream. But no particular human being must choose my dream for me; I have to be the one who defines me, while at the same time I must allow myself to pay close attention to the counsel of individuals who are more experienced about life than I am. Some of such people would be my parents.

President Obama's parents were great dreamers; so is Barack himself. He is very much a results-driven, farsighted leader.

America is a nation of dreams. This is where

Jaytoe Anthony Tukan, Sr.

TURNING OF THE TIDE

one's childhood fantasies most often turn into dreams and realities. Europeans come here; Arabs come here; Asians travel way from the Far East to make it to this land. Many Africans also come here; Mexicans also make it here. For many, many citizens of the world, there is no better land onto which to settle, in order to achieving one's dream. America is the answer for them, even when fleeing for their lives, as they try to avoid prosecution or death, for whatever the reason their native land may have against them. Is anyone really looking for great opportunities? There is no better place can one find greater opportunities than in America.

The President's father had a big, yet seemingly impossible dream. He wanted to be educated in an American university.

From his small Nyanza village in Kenya, he left home to attend college in America in 1959. Immediately settling in Hawaii and enrolling at the University of Hawaii at Manoa, he would study economics. Barack was the first and only African student of the university. This was the civil rights era, and nothing was easy for black people in the United States. Obviously, nothing would be handed on a silver platter to the young African student. What a life Obama truly had ahead of him.

Jaytoe Anthony Tukan, Sr.

TURNING OF THE TIDE

"After long hours of study, my father had joined my grandfather (Gramps) and several other friends at a local Waikiki bar. Everyone was in a festive mood, eating and drinking to the sounds of a slack-key guitar, when a white man abruptly announced to the bartender, loudly enough for everyone to hear, that he shouldn't have to drink good liquor 'next to a nigger,'" Barack writes in his *Dreams from My Father,* about a story his grandfather told him.

All eyes were fastened on Barack's father, as the entire bar was quiet and everybody really thought the African student would start a fight. "Instead, my father stood up, walked over to the man, smiled, and proceeded to lecture him about the folly of bigotry, the promise of the American dream, and universal rights of man," Barack said.

Following such a lecture, the man felt so guilty about his racial remarks that he paid for the food and drinks for everyone at the bar that evening. He gave Obama one hundred dollars, which later paid the young African student's rent for the month. Obama persevered and became more and more focused; he would not throw in the towel and return to Africa.

"From the difficult decision to leave his native

Jaytoe Anthony Tukan, Sr.

TURNING OF THE TIDE

African village to the heart-rending parting from family and friends, we learn to appreciate what it means for a person to undertake the difficult transition from one nation to another. It is a determination in the new immigrant, a determination to succeed regardless of the obstacles, the same kind of determination that has allowed many to overcome the obstacles and succeed."[1]

Obama was more and more determined to achieve his dream of finishing college in America, a land of promise, equality, freedom, opportunity, and justice. After living here for awhile, the President's father must have known very well that life would not be easy. Nevertheless, he was set to fulfill his dream to being educated in America. His unwavering character, despite all kinds of difficulties, helped him to succeed. Why would anyone put a hold on his dream? Why would he give control of his life to another person?

Instead, the young African student persevered even more than ever before. He became more visible on campus, more outspoken, and even spoke on

---

[1]

Dr. James Pula, in his Foreword to (The Other End Of The Tunnel,1998).

Jaytoe Anthony Tukan, Sr.

TURNING OF THE TIDE

behalf of other students. It is also said that he especially stood up for other foreign students. The senior Obama was elected the first president of the International Students Association, of which he was a founding member.

After obtaining his bachelor's degree in economics in June, 1962, he then matriculated to Harvard University, on a scholarship for his graduate study, starting in the Fall of that year. Three years later, he graduated with honors with a master's degree in economics in 1965. So you can see that Mr. Barack Hussein Obama, Sr., stuck to his plan. He was not a quitter.

Jaytoe Anthony Tukan, Sr.

Chapter Two

America Speaks

"One day in the world makes a wealth of difference, and timing is everything;"this was truly a statement from Ms. Janice Ball, my former boss in Washington, D.C. Very frankly, Janice would often advise us, tariff technicians, about the importance of time, as we were inputting into the computer, shipping changes from the Federal Maritime Commission (FMC), dealing with many commodity rates, as those changes had to be done in a timely fashion." Timing is everything."

"Our time has come," an electrifying speech given by Rev. Jesse Jackson at the Democratic National Convention of 1984. But Jesse was not the

Jaytoe Anthony Tukan, Sr.

TURNING OF THE TIDE

Party's choice to face the Republican rival in November, 1984. Mr. Walter Mondale got the nomination.

"Our time has Come," said Jesse that year. So what was Jesse really saying? What did he truly mean? Whose time was he talking about? Black people's time to be in the White House? Time for the minority? Time for a female president? An Hispanic? What was he really talking about?

Then came 1988 when Jesse again energetically campaigned and ran for the presidency. From my own observation of his candidacy, Rev. Jesse Jackson almost came close to being the Party's choice, even though Michael Dukakis was chosen.

Was the 'Our time has come' speech a call and prediction that even though he did not win, the year 1984 was the beginning of an era when an African American would truly be elected president of the United States? Well, while some Americans, black Americans in particular, might have thought Jesse really meant it was time for black people to win the presidency, the point of his speech was very much different and more inclusive. Jesse is an intelligent and broad-minded man, and at such, he could not have given a speech, talking only about black people at a national convention. His speech,

Jaytoe Anthony Tukan, Sr.

TURNING OF THE TIDE

on the contrary, included all Americans. I believe he meant that after four years of President Reagan and the Republicans with nothing good to show for it, it was time for the Democrats to get back into the White House again.

"This administration has made life more miserable for the poor," said Jesse in 1984, about the Ronald Reagan Oval Office. Then he added, "Its policies and programs have been cruel and unfair to working people.... There are now 34 million people in poverty, 15 percent of our nation. 23 million are White; 11 million Black, Hispanic, Asian, and others – mostly women and children."

In all frankness, Rev. Jackson was calling on all Americans: Republicans, Independents, and not only Democrats, to look at the astonishing numbers just mentioned in the preceding paragraph, under Ronald Reagan, and change course; go to the polls on election day in November that year, and elect Walter Mondale, the Democratic candidate for president. Putting the Democrats back into the Oval Office meant a restoration of hope, jobs, and an ease of economic anxiety in the country at the time.

But what about the Rev. Alfred (Al) Charles Sharpton? He ran in 2004, and like Jesse, he was not able to win the Democratic primary. So why

Jaytoe Anthony Tukan, Sr.

TURNING OF THE TIDE

didn't Al or Jesse ever win the U. S. Presidency? Was time not on the side of either men?

Truly, there are Americans who believe that time was not on the side of all the black people who ran for president before Barack Obama. Ask our dear Deborah, a 63-year-old black woman, who said to us: "Not that they (Jesse and Al) were not good men, or didn't have the intellect or the ability, but it's the timing. It's the timing."

Four years after the last black American ran, here comes another candidate, the third African American in recent history, a person with a funny name, Barack Hussein Obama. And what do you know? He wins the United States Presidency.

So it must have been all about timing. For this reason, your humble servant decided to go out to the street corners, marketplaces, and even to the job sites, to dialogue with many, many citizens. Their voices collectively echoed 'timing', that the timing was perfect in 2008 for anyone to win.

"Rev. Jesse Jackson ran twice: 1984 and 1988, but never won. Rev. Al Sharpton also ran in 2004, but did not win. Then Barack Obama ran in 2008 and won. All three are black people. What was the difference this time?" I began the conversation.

Jaytoe Anthony Tukan, Sr.

TURNING OF THE TIDE

Tony, black, about 30 years old, said, "I think, with the war and everything going on with the economy, I think everybody was tired, and ready for a change. He promised change, and so far I think he's doing what he said he was going to do."

Albert, black, about 35 years old, sees it differently. "I mean if you look at it, for most black people in the community, we look at Al Sharpton and Jesse Jackson often times .... they're not going to make the effort to change things. Instead.....they're just talking about it."

In other words, Albert doesn't see those two as having a full agenda for the whole country.

Two black guys, possibly in their early 20s, indicated that Barack was elected to be used as a 'puppy,' in order for them (white people) to get the minority vote, and for Obama to carry on their agenda, not his, but their agenda. As the three of us agreed that it is the U.S. Congress which runs this country, not the president, as the president is only an overseer, one of the fellows remarked, "He's just a representative. It's all behind the paper, and the paper is the Congress."

Jaytoe Anthony Tukan, Sr.

TURNING OF THE TIDE

Anna, white, probably in her late 40's, a lady who seems to be knowledgeable on human behavior and human character, and well on top of economic issues, shared her views with me. "Some of it is timing, I think. I think some of it is the manner in which people carry themselves. .... You can be the right person, but the wrong time, it won't happen."

"And then, maybe people look at somebody like Jesse Jackson as being more militant than Obama is? Is that what you're driving at?" I asked Anna.

"To some extent, yes. But it's not necessarily just the person; it's also who they align themselves with, because that person alone can not possibly do the job. So who do you go to for guidance? Who are you going to look to for grounding? You can't possibly be in all places at all time. ... How are you tapping out and reaching out to people? That is very important. So I don't think it's just any one thing...."

"So you think Obama aligns himself with people of knowledge? I asked Anna again, who so patiently and thoughtfully responded.

"Ultimately..... You still look at how does this person process information? How do they make decision? You can't possibly be so well-rounded and so on top of everything that you are knowledgeable

Jaytoe Anthony Tukan, Sr.

TURNING OF THE TIDE

in all areas,.....” she further indicated.

Ty, a young black lady, possibly 35 years old, shared her views. “I think that we as young people,... knowing that we were able to vote... just not wanting to be heard at that time, or thinking that our votes really count prior to Obama, I think that we were just ready;....... because if you noticed, there were a whole lot of young black people voting.”

“Right,... it had never happened before. Black people don’t usually ever vote” I indicated.

“No! Most of them don’t. I voted for Clinton, though. But yea, I just think that we were ready. I think we wanted to see that change; we were waiting for that change to come. But right now, I think that they are giving him a whole lot of problems because of the fact that he is a black president. And he’s not a quitter, you know. He’s going to continue to fight, whether they want to hear him or not, he’s going to be heard. And I’m behind him one hundred percent. Whatever my president wants, I want,” Ty said.

Tanya, a black woman, maybe in her early 40s, shared her views. “Well, I think it was different for him to win because he went out there himself. He knocked on people’s doors, you know. A lot of

Jaytoe Anthony Tukan, Sr.

politicians, they have people that work for them, get out there and talk for them. He spoke for himself."

"He wasn't afraid to meet the people," I interjected my thought there.

"Exactly! To me that's what made the difference."

Laura and William, a white couple, who may be in their mid 40s, also decided to weigh-in on the election of Obama. Laura said, "I just think that it was the whole... after the Bush Presidency, ... people were ready for a change. People were getting tired..."

"Timing?" I asked Laura.

"Yes, I think so. People were just tired; they wanted a change...... There are the haves and have-nots. There were too many have-nots. We are the ones who pay all the taxes; it's the working class people. I mean, the higher level income......, there's all kinds of tax breaks and tax cuts, tax shelters...."

Laura further indicated that the people in the higher income bracket are those who make the money, and are able to save the money. In other words, the working class people are hit with all kinds of taxes, and therefore have a harder time in finding the way to save money.

Darren and Christie, a black and white couple, with their two beautiful daughters, also shared their views. Darren said "Too much religion involved with Jesse and Al Sharpton. Nobody wanted a preacher; they wanted a president. Back then when they ran, nobody was ready for that."

"So the timing is good for (Obama)," I replied.

He indicated, "The timing is very good. They had no choice.....they had two choices: black man or a woman, the economy (was) so screwed up, it couldn't be any worse. Either way they went, nobody could lose."

Deborah, a 63-year-old black woman, whom I view to be someone with wisdom and parables, also had her saying about the election of Obama. "For one thing, a pill plays a part; a pill plays a parts" she began.

"Okay; how so? I asked Deborah.

"Sharpton and Jesse Jackson, they're from another generation; they're from another generation. So, it's a gap there..... Now I'm 63, so I know what they were like. But you've got to remember what the

TURNING OF THE TIDE

country was like at that time, too. Everything is global now. They (Jesse & Al) were not seen as mainstream. That's my opinion."

"Right, they were not really seen as mainstream, but at the same time, too extreme?" I asked.

"Not mainstream, and too extreme," she seemed to agree... Adding, "Not that they were not good men or didn't have the intellect or the ability. But it's the timing. It's the timing. So now we're in (this) so-called global age. So people are more able to kinda like just pull away from the past, and move forward. And Obama is young, educated, and he is smart."

I followed up again, "And because of that global age, you would think that ... I mean they had another choice. They had Clinton, Hillary Clinton..."

"Well, but when he ran and when men ran for president in the past, it was not all inclusive. Other Americans were not a part of that agenda," said Deborah.

"Okay," I could not help, but to follow and observe, such fascinating statements as coming from the lips of a wise woman, as if she already knew before hand, what were the questions I was going to ask her.

TURNING OF THE TIDE

"So it's just like you wear a pair of (the) same socks every day," she continued, "then you need to change (them) .... To me, if you don't change, you're going to be left behind. For this period of time, he was the best candidate. He was the best candidate."

Cyntavia, black, probably in her early 30s, seemed to be reluctant at first to comment. Later, she said, "I think some of the people's hearts and minds are changing, and wanted a change. It's a change, and more and more people are able to stand up more, to implement that change. They want it..... They want to change; some people want it, and we were able to do more to help it, to get it up and progressing along."

"But that change could have also been carried over by Mrs. Clinton," I tried to remind Cyntavia.

"Yea, it could have, but it just so happened to be appointed by uh.... "

"Why didn't they choose Clinton? Why Obama?" I interrupted Cyntavia.

She quickly replied, "I don't think they're gonna put a female in there too soon." Cyntavia brought a laughter out of me by this statement, as we

Jaytoe Anthony Tukan, Sr.

TURNING OF THE TIDE

both couldn't help ourselves.

"It's gonna take another forty years?" I asked.

"Probably so," she replied.

"So Obama's election was uh.. like a real history making?" I asked Cyntavia.

"Ummh, it was considered history," she agreed.

I went further, "So speaking about history, what do you think history really is, in your mind?"

"In my mind, according to Obama becoming a president? Well, basically what our ancestors fought for years for us to become, to make a difference in the lives of African-Americans. But not just for African Americans, for everybody that didn't really have a say-so, as far as poverty, race, women; just trying to make a difference for changing, another change, ...for history, making it an equal right for each and everyone in the United States," Cyntavia assertively indicated.

"So if Martin Luther King were alive today, and we were talking about this, about Obama being elected president, what (do) you think he would say? How you (do) think he would feel?" I asked her again.

Cyntavia replied, "I would say he may be proud; he may be proud. But once again like he said

Jaytoe Anthony Tukan, Sr.

TURNING OF THE TIDE

in his speech, we still have a long way to go; we still have a long way to go. It didn't change overnight; it took us forty years to make it to this point...."

Johnnie, a black woman, maybe in her early 40s, had this to say. "I believe people were really prepared for a change, and there was not a whole lot of options."

"Hillary was one of the options," I tried to remind Johnnie.

"Hillary? She wasn't," Johnnie objected.

"She is a woman? Is that...?" I tried to ask Johnnie, who seemed to quickly interrupt me, calling me to a point.

"Being that the country was in such a terrible situation, I don't believe people really felt comfortable that a woman could handle the drastic situation that we're facing, with the war and all that. I don't believe that they really felt prepared..."

Of all the people I interviewed, Johnnie was the only person who saw Barack Obama's election from a different angle. She very well attributed it to 'fear' on the part of Americans. Giving war times, citizens only preferred to put the country into the hand of a man, rather than the hand of a woman.

"We claim that we are moving forward to

Jaytoe Anthony Tukan, Sr.

where it could be woman, man, regardless," Johnnie said.

"Regardless, it shouldn't matter, right?" I agreed with Johnnie.

She went on, "Regardless. So it's fear, the bottom line; the bottom line is fear. Fear's still touching the lives of a lot of us. And whether we acknowledge it or not, that's the bottom line. We are in fear of the unknown"

Brian, white, 28 years old, said, "When it comes to the difference between Obama and Jesse Jackson, well, time has changed, I guess. Back then, people were still angry, hurt, scared, and whatever."

"Right, and that's what I'm getting from most everybody I talk to. They say the timing was right for Obama. The timing wasn't on Jesse Jackson's side, or Al Sharpton's side. And there are others that look at Al Sharpton and Jesse to be (a) little more militant than Obama really is," I added.

"Right, I understand," Brian said. "I'm not really big on politics. I don't understand everything in politics, myself. Politics only lets you go so far," Brian further added.

I talked to a young black man, possibly 25 years old. He calls himself 'Big John, who also decided to share his views.

"It depends on who you got; it depends on who you got behind you, who you got on your team. If you ain't got good supporters, you're not gonna win. You see Obama, he already was set before he even started. It depends on how much money you got in your campaign, which they don't say nothing about. So Obama, when he ran,....."

"It was kinda easy," I interjected my views there.

Big John agreed, "It was kinda easy. Jesse Jackson and Al Sharpton, they're out front;..they're like for a movement, not for president. They look at them like that. They're good for marches, not for president.

Dean, a black lady, probably 40 years old, said that Obama won partly because Oprah was behind him. In other words, when Oprah is in your corner, you are gone.

"But you have to also remember, Jesse did what Jesse did, and Al does what Al does; they are very voiceful. But the president, he's silent, but he's got a big throne. He's strong, very strong. Character, character makes it. He's got wisdom, got lots of wisdom.....," she said.

TURNING OF THE TIDE

Dean indicated that Jesse and Al "don't have that ruling power. They speak, but they want what? Someone else to move for them. The President, he speaks, and everybody runs. Everybody gets their second. They know which way to go. But he's already set them up and talked to them, and said, you know what? I want you, you, and you; this is what I want. He didn't have to change his mind. And he didn't have to tell them the second time."

A black lady, possibly 26 years old, who decided to remain anonymous, also said, like Dean, that Oprah was in Obama's corner, and that made a big difference.

Additionally, she said, "I just think it's about marketing yourself. He sold himself well, and the fact that he's half-white, that played a part."

Ms. Anonymous went on to say that Obama's competitor, John McCain, was too old to go against a younger man. "Not articulate, he couldn't really express himself thoroughly."

"He is a full military valor of honor. I mean, who would be a better commander-in-chief? Somebody who has been in the military. You would think John McCain would have been a better

Jaytoe Anthony Tukan, Sr.

TURNING OF THE TIDE

commander-in-chief," I told her.

Ms. Anonymous replied, "First of all, he looks like he's about to fall over. How do you know he would have lived for four years? I mean, barely, his arguments, they weren't as strong as Obama's. He hardly even had a fighting chance," she said.

Sharon, probably in her late 20s, shared her views as well...."I think Jesse probably puts his hand in too many places very quickly. .... Sometimes he's budding in too much, where I feel like ... leave it alone," she said. Going further, Sharon observed, "Obama kinda looks at all facts and gathers all information, and sometimes he doesn't get involved. Jesse just jumps in (too fast) before he realizes, and then he jumps back out. He is too political! So I think that's why (he did not win)."

I then introduced to Sharon some of Big John's statements, when he said, that Jesse and Al are good in mobilizing people, same way Martin Luther King was. She agreed, but had to differ a little bit, by indicating that King would have been a president had he lived.

I had to wonder about that. What is the major difference between what Al & Jesse do and stand for today, and what Martin did and stood for yesterday?

Jaytoe Anthony Tukan, Sr.

TURNING OF THE TIDE

Why would it be probable for Martin to become president, but not Jesse or Al?

Elizabeth, black, in her mid 50s, shared her thoughts on that. "King was different. Jesse is not as brave as Martin was. Martin could take risks, as long as he knew that what he was doing was the right thing for everyone. It did not matter if someone threatened his life or not, he would continue to fight on. Jesse is also brave, but not that brave to the point of risking his life like Martin."

"So it seems to me, Barack is somewhat like Martin. He seems to be a risk taker. I mean, there had been attempts on his life, even when he was running for president, but that did not stop him," I said to Elizabeth.

"Yes, Barack is like Martin. He's brave to the point of risking his life; he's brave enough to go on, regardless the cost."

David, white, about mid 40s, indicated to us, "I don't know. I try to think, Jesse Jackson? I don't know too much about him.... Al Sharpton? To be honest with you, anything (that) comes out of his mouth, everything (that) comes out of that man's mouth, is to me, affronts to everything I believe in, and everything I believe that Afro-Americans would

Jaytoe Anthony Tukan, Sr.

believe in. Not quite sure if I've said that right."

I was a little baffled by this statement, but David decided to clarify what he meant.

"Give me any example of anything he said, and I'll tell you, I don't understand why he's saying that. Anything I've ever heard him speak on TV, and I say, how can he be a leader of any group.., of any race? I can't understand why anybody would follow this man. Now Obama, on the other hand, he's a liberal, a left-wing liberal. I happen to be a right-wing conservative. But, a lot of people believe in his platform, his thoughts. It don't make any difference what color...."

"Umm,.. so that's why he won; somebody told me that they (Jesse & Al) can start a movement; they are good in mobilizing people. But, if made a leader, they wouldn't know what to do," I said. Continuing, "One white lady gave me an example, 'Obama will not be the one, if something happens to a black kid in North Carolina (racially speaking).. ... he would just jump on the bus or on the plane to come here, and try to help out'......."

David interjected, "But Al Sharpton would do that. He's out here fighting for a cause......,environment, financial overview....."

Tiffany,18, the youngest of all the people

interviewed, commented. "I think they were looking for someone...I don't think they wanted Hillary."

"Hillary is white; it was a better choice (for the norm, in our society)," I tried to suggest to the young lady.

Tiffany immediately replied, "But she's a woman."

"She's a woman? Well, are you saying no woman......"

Tiffany comes back, "I think it would have been better if she would have won. But I think that America don't want women right now."

I asked Tiffany if she was old enough during the last election to vote. She said she was not 18 at the time, but "I'm 18 now."

I then encouraged Tiffany that she will get her chance to vote starting the next election, Obama's second term.

As you have read, many people shared the same views about why Obama won the election. Taking no credit away from candidate Obama, they all` agreed that he is qualified to be president. However, since the country was in such a terrible, economic condition, this helped him greatly. To put it very concisely, the timing was right for anyone to win, Hillary or Barack.

Chapter Three

BEARING THE TORCH

They come in different ways, and from different geographical parts of the world. They may look different, but they all have a single agenda. Some of them are born in places where there is no sign of mosquitoes; for the rest of them, their birthplaces are infested with nothing but mosquitoes and malaria. Some are born in the hospital, while others are truly, truly born on a farmland.

Some leaders are really born, while others are made. The color of their skin may be very different. Nonetheless, there is only a single purpose in life for them: to brighten the lives of others, and to make a significant difference in the lives of other people.

Sometimes they sacrifice all that others may truly succeed. For them, there is no need to live if

Jaytoe Anthony Tukan, Sr.

TURNING OF THE TIDE

those around them will be in bondage; life has no meaning if the people living next door are not allowed to breathe the free air which is given to the universe by the Almighty God. For them, freedom is a right that everyone must have, regardless the race, creed, nationality/ethnicity, or religion. Those are *torch bearers,* leaders who would shape the course of our destiny. About those leaders, living or dead, history is being made, and history will forever be written. While all leaders may not necessarily be torch bearers, personally, I believe that **all** torch bearers are leaders. We recognize a few *heroes* as *torch bearers.*

Mrs. Rosa Parks is one of our torch bearers. She was quiet, yet very steadfast, spoke very softly and silently, but her quiet voice, not only did it change her town, her city, the entire community, it also changed a whole nation.

Jaytoe Anthony Tukan, Sr.

TURNING OF THE TIDE

Rosa Louise McCauley, the first child of James McCauley and Leona Edwards, was born in Tuskegee, Alabama, on February 4, 1913. While James worked as a carpenter, Leona was a school teacher. Rosa had a younger brother, Sylvester.

The family later moved to Pine Level, near Montgomery, Alabama, where Rosa was home-schooled by her mother until she was eleven years old. Her mother then enrolled Rosa at the Montgomery Industrial School for Girls. Perhaps with the desire to follow her mother's footsteps as a teacher, Rosa enrolled at the Alabama State Teachers College for Negroes, after passing to the 11th grade.

Unfortunately grandmother Rose Edwards, seriously became ill and later passed away. It was a devastating blow for Rosa; she had to stop her schooling for awhile. As she was about ready to resume classes, her mother also became ill. With one incident after another, Rosa had to suspend her schooling indefinitely in order to care for her mother. Rosa's younger brother, Sylvester, had to find work to meet up with some of the family's obligations.

Rosa and Raymond Parks were married on December 18, 1932. Though his actual date of birth

45   **Jaytoe Anthony Tukan, Sr.**

TURNING OF THE TIDE

is really not known to us, Raymond was born in Wedowee, Alabama, in 1903. Due to the racial segregation of schools, he did not receive any formal education. But this did not stop Raymond from learning while he could. He educated himself very well at home, through a great motherly guidance and encouragement from his mother, Geri Parks. He read a lot, and became so knowledgeable of domestic affairs and current events in such a way that many thought he was a college graduate. However, Raymond never went to college.

With Raymond's strong support to his wife's education, Mrs. Parks returned to school and eventually received her high school diploma in 1934, about two years after their marriage. She was 21 years old.

Raymond and his wife were active members of the National Association for the Advancement of Colored People (NAACP). Rosa served as secretary and youth leader of the local Montgomery branch.

Another 21 years after high school, Rosa would make a decision on December 1,1955, on her way from work. Perhaps unaware at the time the effect or impact this would have on her personally, such a decision did not only change her life, but it did surprisingly and forever change the course of

Jaytoe Anthony Tukan, Sr.

TURNING OF THE TIDE

history in the United States.

At 42 years old, Mrs. Rosa Parks finally had enough of the oppression, humiliation, and discrimination by a segregated white society against black people. She did explain in her book, *Quiet Strength*, regarding what truly went down that day.

"On Thursday evening, December 1, I was riding the bus home from work. A white man got on, and the driver looked our way and said, "'Let me have those seats.'"

Rosa did not think it was proper for a woman to give up her seat to a man. She, therefore, refused to stand up. Besides, there was this double injustice that Rosa could not stand. The row in which she and the other three black passengers were sitting had already been designated for 'colored people.' At first, all four black passengers did not move. Then the bus driver again demanded.

"Y'all better make it light on yourselves and let me have those seats."

Three of the black passengers stood up, but Rosa refused to get up. Rather, she decided to move near the window, making room for the white passenger to sit. The white passenger, nevertheless, did not want to sit, even though there were three

Jaytoe Anthony Tukan, Sr.

TURNING OF THE TIDE

seats available in that row. I have to wonder. Was that row not clean enough because a black passenger was still sitting there? Or, did the white passenger and Blake, the bus driver, want to rub Rosa's nose into the mud? Was this another way of exhibiting their white supremacy? Truly, they decided that day, like every other day, to exercise once again their superior power by all means necessary. Rosa herself wondered about that.

"Our mistreatment was just not right, and I was tired of it. The more we gave in, the worse they treated us. I kept thinking about my mother and my grandparents, and how strong they were. I knew there was a possibility of being mistreated, but an opportunity was being given to me to do what I had asked of others. I knew someone had to take the first step. So I made up my mind not to move."

Blake, the bus driver, was also tired of Rosa's refusal to stand up or get off the bus. He called in the police,and Rosa was arrested.

Mrs. Parks, a very strong member of the African Methodist Episcopal Church, said later, "I felt the Lord would give me the strength to endure whatever I had to face. God did away with all my fear. It was time for someone to stand up – or in my case, sit down. I refused to move."

Jaytoe Anthony Tukan, Sr.

TURNING OF THE TIDE

The courageous action of Rosa, which led to her arrest and detention, got the attention of black people in Montgomery. They quickly mobilized and formed the Montgomery Improvement Association (MIA). The MIA elected the young preacher on the block, Pastor of the Dexter Avenue Baptist Church, Dr. Martin Luther King, Jr., to be its president and spokesperson. As a pastor, Dr. King did not ascribe to protesting and demonstrating through violence; instead, he advocated and encouraged a nonviolent movement. Under his leadership, black people decided to boycott the city bus line. For over a year, approximately 381days in counting, black people somehow found their own way either to work, or any other place where they needed to be. Montgomery bus transportation system was paralyzed, and the city lost big revenue for this reason. In addition to this boycott, many, many brave people of all races came and demanded equal rights for all. The bus boycott did not end until December 21, 1956, when the U.S. Supreme Court declared that it was unconstitutional to segregate on the bus.

A torch bearer is a leader, plus more. A torch bearer looks beyond himself/herself and sees a much bigger picture. Bearing the torch involves risk taking. In this specific situation, Mrs. Rosa Parks

Jaytoe Anthony Tukan, Sr.

TURNING OF THE TIDE

looked beyond herself and appropriately acted, or one might actually say, inappropriately acted; it simply did not matter what the consequence would be to her personal being. So we choose Mrs. Rosa Parks as one of the **torch bearers** in this book. Because of her action, improvements were made regarding the treatment of black people in the United States.

Yet, the tide wouldn't let down; it continued to rise and rise. Though change was coming to black people, there was no turning of the tide. Black people still had a long, long way to go.

I wonder what was on the minds of some of black people of the civil rights days. I believe many of them were asking, like Martin Luther King, Jr., "How long, God? When will we see the light?"

But there was that light at 'the other end of the tunnel.' Black people needed to hang in there a little while longer.

Jaytoe Anthony Tukan, Sr.

Ask me to go on a trip with you and show you a farsighted, unshakeable, persistent, and most patient leader, I will take you to Dexter Avenue Baptist Church in Montgomery, Alabama, where the pastor will greet us at the door with love, humility and kindness. Then ask me to show you someone, who could be revered as a great leader with all the glory and untold riches the world could offer him, yet he would turn away from the  riches and glory, and would rather teach his friends and enemies, the simplicity of love.

If you want me to show you a person, who would remind us all that glorification belongs to God, I will take you to the home of a lady called Coretta, to speak to her husband and the father of her four children. Even if we did not meet this loving father home, we would still rest assured that he was on the other side of town, trying "to help someone who is traveling wrong," in his own words.

Even if you and I went after him to the other side of town, but were told that he had just flown to Philadelphia, Mississippi, because there were many

Jaytoe Anthony Tukan, Sr.

TURNING OF THE TIDE

reports of racial tension and police brutality, that conditions could escalate, and so many lives might be lost. And if we went back to the house to talk to his wife about this, we would be assured by Coretta that everything would be all right once he was there. Even if you and I had the money to fly after him to Mississippi, and as we got there, we would be asking ourselves: 'where is the commotion that everybody was talking about? Where is the police brutality?' We would be amazed that there was no commotion, no police brutality, none at all, because he had already spoken to all those involved, reminding everybody about his nonviolent approach to solving racial injustice and inequality. As usual, he would have already encouraged patience by black people.

Then and only then - would you need not ask me any more to show you someone, because you would have known that he was that leader, the **torch bearer**, who knew how to calm the crowd. When he spoke, all would listen. That's the leader, the servant, the man, who would fight nonviolently, even to the death, to make the wrong right, to set the crooked places straight, to tell America's white society that, if one American is not free, all Americans are not free. To say over and again, if a

TURNING OF THE TIDE

single American is denied access to a movie theater unless that person went through a door designated for colored people, then all Americans are still in bondage.

You would not ask me any longer, to show you somebody. Rather, you, yourself would be amazed about who he really was, because you would have seen how calm everyone was as the people listened to him. Then you and I would believe as his wife had told us that 'everything would be all right once he (Martin) was there.'

Martin Luther King, Jr., was born on January 15, 1929, in Atlanta, Georgia, unto Rev. Martin Luther King, Sr., and Alberta Williams King. Martin's father was born 'Michael King', and the son was initially named after his father. At five years old, little Michael and his family traveled to Europe in 1934 and visited Germany. His father changed both names to Martin Luther, in honor of the Late German Protestant, who was excommunicated from the Roman Catholic Church.

When Rosa Parks disobeyed the bus driver's order by refusing to stand up for a white man to sit in the colored people's row on December 1, 1955, a 26-year-old young Baptist minister had just become

Jaytoe Anthony Tukan, Sr.

TURNING OF THE TIDE

pastor of the Dexter Avenue Baptist Church, Montgomery, Alabama. Martin was one of the black people who mobilized and formed the Montgomery Improvement Association (MIA). He was elected president and spokesman for the group, not only to fight for the freedom of Rosa, then in police custody, but also to plan a boycott of the city buses.

Besides being a pastor who did not cater to violence, it is believed that King grew up in a middle class neighborhood in Atlanta, Geogia, where some of his friends were white. What would be his quarrel with those white friends if he were to lead a violent revolution against white people? Instead, King advocated a nonviolent approach in fighting racism and injustice. But little did he know at the time that the bus boycott incident, the mobilization of the people, and the formation of the MIA, would really set in motion for his gaining prominence, not only in Montgomery, but also on the national scene.

King attended the Booker T. Washington High School in Atlanta, but skipped the 9th grade. While still in the 11th grade, King took the entrance exam for Morehouse College, and did score highly on the exam. Therefore, there was no reason or restriction for him not to enter college right away.

Jaytoe Anthony Tukan, Sr.

TURNING OF THE TIDE

He was admitted, and started classes at age 15. It was three years later when King, at 18, graduated with a bachelor's degree in Sociology in 1948. He matriculated to Crozer Theological Seminary in Chester, Pennsylvania, for his graduate work. After receiving his master's degree in Divinity in 1951, he then enrolled at Boston University and began his doctorate studies in Systematic Theology. King received his doctorate degree on June 5, 1955.

As God would have it, the completion of King's education, and his acceptance of the head pastoral position at the Dexter Avenue Baptist Church, could not have been more timely for the 26-year-old young pastor, as this coincided with the refusal of Rosa Parks to stand up or get off the bus. Did God really prepare the young minister for the task ahead? Did King see this coming early on? Did he envision that God actually got him ready at the right time to do His will?

History will speak for itself that baby King was born for this reason: to help his country, the 'evil America' to see its wrongs and the many injustices to its citizens, and perhaps change course. Brave to the point of risking his life, and the safety of his family, regardless how many death threats were directed at him and his family, Martin would

Jaytoe Anthony Tukan, Sr.

not give up hope that some day, his people, and all peoples in America, and the free world, would see the light. So we have chosen Dr. Martin Luther King, Jr., as a great **torch bearer** for our story.

Sidney Poitier defied all odds, and broke through Hollywood's strong racial barriers, to become one of the best movie stars the world has ever known. The sky was the limit as to how far he could reach. Before Sidney's emergence as an actor, many blacks in America who exhibited acting talents and skills, were seen for the most part, as entertainers and servants, not movie stars. It is not that black  people did not have the natural talents to act and play leading roles. But it was still a fact that, even in the movies, America still saw everything in black and white, as it did in real life.

But there was a new kid on the block who would demand racial equality as well. He did that with talents, styles, charisma, together with his ability and unwavering character to demand the

Jaytoe Anthony Tukan, Sr.

portraying of leading roles, as he played the screen to that end. Mr. Poitier is known as one of the first black actors to hold the torch, traveling through the rugged road to Hollywood, leading and paving the way for would-be black actors and actresses we see on the big screen today. Nevertheless, life did not start out for him that way. From the very beginning, it was an uphill battle, and nothing would be handed on a silver platter to Sidney.

~~~~~~~~~~~~~~~~~~~~~~~~~~~~~

Somehow you were born on a tropical land, an island, in a tiny little town, quite small, so everyone knows everybody else. You are growing up in a thatched-roofed house, no electricity, on a land where a glimpse of hope for the future is ever dim. You are ten years old, still young, but your parents want the best for you. They think by getting you out of that small town, perhaps moving you to the capital city, you may have a better future.

Yet the parents will soon find out that the capital city is very much different from the village where you were born. There is that class-system which introduces itself to them early on: the haves and the have-nots. The former includes those who are living well, or have a much better life than you

TURNING OF THE TIDE

do, while the latter includes people who are just surviving.

At ten years old, you seem very lost, and wonder how to find your way. You miss your friends, left behind on that little island, or in that small town. A few of your friends may be jealous, while many are happy that you have moved on to a better life. But the reality is that life is not as easy to live in that big city, your new residence, as it was in that tiny place, a village you once called home; home you so love, yet had to leave behind. What do you do? Would you turn around to go back? Even though you are so young to understand all this, you know your parents want the best for you.

Additionally, you know them very well, too, that once they have made that move, there's no turning back. They (all of you) are going to stay put. Do you run away? Where to?

Yet those who do not know you, or do not know about how your life has begun and evolved, do admire you, as you excel in life, whether in the government, a corporate setting, or within the legal environment (maybe you are a dynamic lawyer), or you've found your place on the big screen. They admire you very, very well.

On the big screen, playing a leading role, a

Jaytoe Anthony Tukan, Sr.

TURNING OF THE TIDE

good guy? Your admirers watch and love you to death. Never mind how you have struggled, or how you got here. Never mind who has helped you, or who refused to help you to make it this far. But they only see you because you are now here, - in the present. They like this hero, this role model that they see in you; your admirers love this guy, and would pay the ducats[2] to see him over and over again.

At first there is the industry, the big industry, itself, that is - Hollywood, whose executives would have nothing to do with you. Why would they? You do not belong in their circle. No, you don't look like any of them. Your people are not a part of that power establishment. So why should they accept you? You are on your own.

But your value system, that great value system, which was instilled in you by your parents in that little village, that upbringing you have received from most everybody in that small town, does not only live within you, it is you. It has become who you really are. In all honesty, you are truly a person, whose will-power is very strong and so rooted,

---

[2]

(**Ducats**, in Shakespearean days, meant money, the bucks, or greenbacks).

Jaytoe Anthony Tukan, Sr.

TURNING OF THE TIDE

nothing will deter you from anything to which you firmly set your mind. You must work to succeed, as you are now in the greatest of countries in the world, a country where one's dreams come true, a place where anything, perhaps everything, is possible. For you, failure is not one of the options on the table. No, not at all! This is how you see yourself. There are no excuses! No short cuts! You must persevere!

~~~~~~~~~~~~~~~~~~

Originally from Cat Island, Bahamas, baby Sidney was born at sea, unto Reginald James and Evelyn Poitier, on February 20, 1927, on a vessel en-route to Miami, Florida, as his parents, both tomato farmers, were going to sell tomatoes at the Produce Exchange Market. Premature at birth, and barely weighing three pounds, his father resigned himself to the fact that the baby would only live for a few days. Mr. Poitier said in: *The Measure of a Man:* "My father, who had lost several children already to disease and stillbirth, was somewhat stoical about the situation. He went to a local undertaker in the "colored" section of Miami to prepare for my burial, coming home with a shoebox that could serve as a miniature casket. My mother, however, felt that I could be saved."

Jaytoe Anthony Tukan, Sr.

TURNING OF THE TIDE

Sidney's mother paid a visit to a soothsayer to consult with her. For a charge of fifty cents, the soothsayer said, "Don't worry about your son. He will survive and he will not be a sickly child ......He will travel to most of the corners of the earth. He will walk with kings. He will be rich and famous. Your name will be carried all over the world. You must not worry about that child." Sidney's mother told her husband that their child would live.

Sidney spent his early childhood on Cat Island, Bahamas, until he was 10, when the family moved to Nassau, the Bahamian capital. He did not start his schooling until around 11 years old, but did not stay in school either. He was out at 13. In Nassau, life was really different and confusing for Sidney. At 15, his parents shipped him to his older brother, Cyril, in Miami, Florida.

So there was Sidney living with his brother in Miami. Somehow Miami had reminded him a little of Nassau, his own capital city, as there were some similarities. Like Nassau, with a class-system: the haves and the have-nots, Miami had its prejudices, much more so rigid on racial lines. He was glad to be with his brother in that city, but was the city of Miami ready to accept Sidney within its limits?

Sidney explained his ordeal one day when he

Jaytoe Anthony Tukan, Sr.

TURNING OF THE TIDE

tried to pick up his clothes from the dry cleaners. He was told the clothes were not ready, but since he needed the clothes for the following morning, they suggested to him to go to their head office, located at the other side of town. He took the bus there, only to find out that the clothes were not ready. But that other side of town was the white people's side of town. To make matter worse for him, the city bus system had shut down for the night. And there he was trying to hitchhike to the other side, the colored people's side of town. What a situation he found himself in.

But Sidney put his thumb up for the wrong car: an unmarked police vehicle. The officer who sat in the passenger seat ordered him into the alley. He obeyed the cop's order, and walked through the alley, as they drove behind him.

"There was no one else around. Whatever happened, there would be no witnesses," Sidney indicated.

As the police car pulled up behind him, the driver rolled down the window and pulled out his revolver. "What should we do with this boy? Find out what he's doing over here. Should we shoot him here?" Sidney could hear the officers deciding whether to end his life right there, or first find out

Jaytoe Anthony Tukan, Sr.

TURNING OF THE TIDE

what his mission was in the neighborhood at that time.

After telling the officers why he was there, Sidney Poitier was given another chance to live. "Boy, if we let you go, you think you can walk all the way home without looking back once?" The officer on the wheel asked him.

"Yes, sir," Poitier replied.

"Think about it now,..cuz if you look back, just once, we gonna shoot you," he was warned.

Wow! You don't say; talk about fellow human beings deciding your life right in front of you without any compassion or sensitivity at all. Poitier walked fifty long blocks home without once looking back! Fifty (50) long blocks for a kid to walk?

Other incidents happened after this one, and Sidney Poitier had his share of trouble in Miami; it was clear that enough was enough. He decided to run away from the South, heading North. His brother, Cyril, with a wife and six children had no time to go chasing after a runaway teenager, who should have kept himself out of trouble in the first place.

Mr. Poitier found himself within the great surroundings of the Big Apple, and life was more

Jaytoe Anthony Tukan, Sr.

TURNING OF THE TIDE

livable in New York than it was for him in Miami. But the city presented its own very dark shadows through which he must travel in order to survive. From my own experience for the few months I spent in New York, it is always a city which seems to welcome everybody, but New York City is 'no man's land.'

Firstly, Sidney finds himself in the midst of a riot, and got shot in the leg; he had to lie and play dead in order to live. Otherwise, any movement from him would have been answered by another bullet to finish him off. Secondly, there was the job site, where some of Sidney's dishwashing co-workers did not make life any easier for him, as one of them pulled out a knife and almost slashed his throat. All of this added more pressure to the stressful life he already had ahead of him.

Personally, it is my feeling that he realized later on, and perhaps appreciated the fact that bad as these incidents were, they were necessary, in order to put him on his guard early on. He needed to know that though he was no longer in Miami, New York City was no Cat Island, either. He had to learn fast, and very fast.

Scrambling on hotdogs in New York, and going through a terrible winter for the first time,

Jaytoe Anthony Tukan, Sr.

TURNING OF THE TIDE

Sidney had to settle for the U.S. Army. But the army and Sidney could not see eye-to-eye with each other; an immediate separation was imminent. How would it come about? That was the major question. When he realized that the army would not be the first to make this happen, Poitier took matters into his own hands. Over a little disagreement, he would throw a chair at a superior officer, only for the chair to miss, crashing into a glass window. He was sent for a psychiatric evaluation. According to the army, he was very insane to commit such an act. Sidney had no disagreement on the insanity charge; his unsolicited wish was therefore granted. He was thrown out of the army.

After the army, Mr. Poitier would try his hand in acting. A chance came for him to audition at the American Negro Theater for Broadway, but the audience could not relate to his heavy Bahamian accent, as the whole place was in an uproar with laughter. Poitier would use the next six months in teaching himself standard English, as he listened to radio announcers, following their diction, in an effort to perfecting himself. This paid off very well, as the producer and the audience heard a different Poitier, when he got another chance at the same theater. This time he made it, and became a cast

Jaytoe Anthony Tukan, Sr.

TURNING OF THE TIDE

member of a Broadway show, **Lysistrata,** in 1946. His great performance on Broadway paved the way for a movie deal in **No Way *Out***, which created another opportunity in **The Blackboard Jungle** in 1955, followed by **The Defiant Ones,** which would actually move the handsome and charismatic actor into stardom. For this movie, Mr. Poitier received an American Academy nomination in 1958. Though he did not win, as the award went to his white co-actor, Tony Curtis, this was a great progress for him, somebody from a small island, where a hope for any bright future was very unlikely. This was also great for Poitier, who could not even speak English well, when he first entered an English speaking society.

In 1963, Poitier would star in *The Lilies of the Field*, for which he made history, by becoming the first black to win an **Oscar** for Best Actor. The other black male actor before Poitier was James Baskett, who received an Honorary **Oscar** for his role as Uncle Remus in **Song of the South** in 1948. Before both men, a black actress, Ms. Hattie McDaniel, won an **Oscar** for Best Supporting Actress in 1939, for her role in **Gone with the Wind.**

Mr. Poitier made many other movies, such as, *A Patch of Blue*, which the actor described as "one

Jaytoe Anthony Tukan, Sr.

TURNING OF THE TIDE

of the best artworks" he has ever done, attributing that success to his fellow cast members. In 1967, he became the best movie star in America for his roles in three separate movies: *To Sir, With Love, In The Heat Of The Night,* and *Guess Who's Coming to Dinner.*

For his perseverance, charisma, together with his styles, and ability to play the screen to that end, Sidney became one of the few great black actors who paved the way to Hollywood for other black actors and actresses we see on the big screen today. So we choose Mr. Sidney Poitier as a great **torch bearer** in our story

~~~~~~~~~~~~~~~~~~~~

Besides being an actor, Mr. Poitier is a great humanitarian. He was one of 16 well-distinguished personalities who were awarded the Presidential Medal of Freedom on August 12, 2009. Presenting the nation's highest civilian honor from the White House Grounds to the recipients, President Barack Obama told the nation:

"This is a chance for me and for the United States of America to say thank you to some of the finest citizens of this country and of all countries.

"At a moment when cynicism and doubt too

Jaytoe Anthony Tukan, Sr.

TURNING OF THE TIDE

often prevail, when our obligations to one another are too often forgotten, when the road ahead can seem too long or hard to tread, these extraordinary men and women, these agents of change, remind us that excellence is not beyond our abilities, that hope lies around the corner and that justice can still be won in the forgotten corners of this world.

"They remind us that we each have it within our powers to fulfill dreams, to advance the dreams of others and to remake the world for our children," the President indicated.

Some of those honored besides Mr. Poitier, were Archbishop Desmond Tutu of South Africa, and Sandra Day O'Connor, U.S. Supreme Court Associate Justice, to name but a few.

Poitier has six children, four by his first wife, Juanita Hardy. Their marriage lasted from April 29, 1950 until 1965. He is now married to Joanna Shimkus from Canada, since January 23, 1976. His children are: Beverly, Pamela, Sherri, Anika, Sydney and Tamiia.

Jaytoe Anthony Tukan, Sr.

Chapter Four

The Beginning

They were doing fine and very happy in their land. In their communities, little boys always look up to their big brothers, while little girls also look up to the older sisters in the family. Among them, you will never find a perfect family, but they talk about their problems, and resolve them as quickly as possible. As for community training, the older children always step up to the plate by helping their parents to train the younger siblings, in addition to being the protectors for the little ones, among other duties.

The continent comprises of so many countries, sub-divided into so many tribes. A group of citizens or families constitutes a tribe, speaking the same or similar dialect. Within a given town are many sub-divisions, which some may call Quarters. Tribal

Jaytoe Anthony Tukan, Sr.

members in each of those Quarters always protect their own.

Among them, we see Clans, composed of so many tribes, towns, kinsmen and townsmen. Depending on the African nation and its laws, each town may choose or elect someone, usually a man, called the Town Chief. A group of Clans gets together to elect a Clan Chief. A council of chiefs would gather to choose candidates for the highest office of the Clans, and from among the candidates, all Clans will then elect a Paramount Chief. So, when you look at the tribal hierarchy in some parts of Africa, you see the Paramount Chief at the top, the Clan Chief, down to the Town Chief. This was the political structure; when kinsmen had issues, those were the leaders to whom they would go. Africans did not need anyone, an outsider, to interfere with their peace and tranquility.

Africans were always unique in their land, but there is one big problem that Africans have: they love strangers. They love people from outside their continent. Some Africans even help strangers more than they help their own blood brothers and sisters.

So you may ask: if Africans are doing good deeds by helping other people, why could that be a problem? This is a problem because some of these strangers turn around and hurt the Africans. Quite often, strangers take advantage of the good nature of Africans, and before the Africans realize that they have given a helping hand too much so soon, sometimes it is already too late to turn back the clock. The price the Africans pay for this may be too costly to bear.

They were very, very proud to be where God planted them: on the African Continent. Most Africans, if not all Africans, consider it a blessing to be an African. If there were issues, kinsmen always gathered to resolve their conflict. Outsiders were not invited to solve problems for them. There sometimes were bigger conflicts between towns, certainly among African Clans, due, in part, to territorial boundaries, or a dispute over the ownership of a piece of land. Other times the conflicts may extend beyond countries, a dispute of some sort, between two African countries. If it became impossible to find any resolution by negotiations, the two nations would challenge each other on a battlefield as a way of resolving the conflict. Africans did not need strangers to settle their palaver. That's the way life was for the Africans.

You also see royalty; yes, you will see true royalty in some African nations. There are the

Jaytoe Anthony Tukan, Sr.

TURNING OF THE TIDE

African Kings, Queens, Princes, and the African princesses. So it was on the African Continent. Then one day, somebody came to town: a stranger.

Due to their love for strangers, the Africans welcomed the stranger in. The Town Chief and his elders got together to demand the mission of the stranger, who said he was a businessman in search for gold, and willing to trade for some of his "greenbacks." Yes, the African Continent is very, very rich with gold, cobalt, and other minerals, together with plenty of crops. What businessman will hear of the richness of the continent, and will not want to trade with the Africans? The stranger was given a place outside the main town to settle in. As the place was still uncultivated, the Africans cut down the trees, cut the grass, and built a house, not anything like the huts they lived in. It was a real house, designed by the stranger himself. So the businessman had settled in permanently. The place given to the stranger was named a 'white community.' Let it be known, my dear reader, that there was not such a label or name ever assigned to any of the African communities until that day. This was the first sign of discrimination against the Africans, by the Africans themselves, in favor of the stranger. Would you really blame the stranger for

Jaytoe Anthony Tukan, Sr.

this? No, by their own choosing, the Africans did this to themselves. Nobody else to blame but the Africans themselves.

The stranger hired men to go digging into the African rich waters for gold. And what was the pay for those strong African men and boys who helped the stranger? Well, if I told you, some of you might get so angry and trash this book. I do not want to deprive you from reading the rest of the story. You've got to finish reading it to really know what went down. However, whatever the amount the workers received, it was of significant value in those days.

Then one day, probably six months later, something happened. Surprisingly, another stranger came to town. Who was he? The first stranger, losing no time, summoned the Town Chief and his elders to the 'white community,' and introduced the second stranger as his brother. Can you imagine that?

"What is his mission?" One of the elders asked. The Town Chief interpreted to the first stranger, demanding an immediate answer.

"My brother is a messenger of God," the first stranger replied. So his brother was a missionary, who would introduce someone to the Africans,

TURNING OF THE TIDE

someone called the Supreme God of the universe. Many of the elders became apprehensive about this one.

"What other gods can there be? We have our own gods," some of the elders said to their chief. Yes, some of the Africans in that day, worshiped the trees, the moon, and the stars. They also worshiped gods of the earth, who would tell them before any farming season, whether or not, their farms for that year were going to produce plenty of crops. Even today in some African countries, citizens still carry on these tribal or ethnic rituals.

The elders asked the two strangers to leave their presence, as they were going to tête-à-tête on this matter and make a decision. After about a half an hour, the two strangers were then summoned back into the meeting room. "We do not need any other gods," the spokesman for the elders echoed the will of all the elders present. As he was about to announce the decision to send the second stranger back home, to wherever his home was, the first stranger stood up and pleaded with the Town Chief and the elders to kindly allow his brother to stay. He offered them some 'greenbacks' and some African cola he had purchased in preparation for the occasion. The elders calmed down, made peace, and

Jaytoe Anthony Tukan, Sr.

allowed the second stranger to indefinitely settle in.

Dear reader, I want you to bear with me, and patiently imagine with me now, without being bored, that this incident of strangers arriving on the African Continent without prior notice, had continued for years. The next arrivals were the wives and children of the first two strangers; then some in-laws also arrived. So many cousins and their families would also set foot on the African soil. More missionaries, as some did consider themselves to be, continued to appear. The 'white community' you can imagine now, had gotten bigger and bigger.

Visualize for just a moment that this very influx of strangers setting foot on the African Continent continued in many African nations, not just a few. Instead of us looking at a simple white community, the Africans would see their society completely turning into so many white communities in many, many African nations. The African Continent is now at this point so populated with strangers.

The Africans have themselves to blame for this unnecessary influx and settlement of strangers all over the African Continent. This is what the kindness and hospitality of the Africans did to the Africans. No stranger to blame here.

"What other gods can there be? We have our own gods," some of the elders said to their chief.

Chapter Five

Lynching

Tribalism, which is a form of discrimination, exists on the continent. Tribalism is when a person from a given tribe, or a group of individuals think they are superior, and should be the only people to get all the opportunities in the land.

Tribalism? Yes! Slavery? No! There was no sign of slavery until the continent got so populated with strangers.

Some of those strangers claimed to be businessmen. If they were true businessmen, some had forsaken businesses at home, home which would later be known as the New World. Those strangers had partners still living in the New World; those partners, being forsaken, needed workers, to help cultivate their farms, the cotton farms or plantations.

Jaytoe Anthony Tukan, Sr.

TURNING OF THE TIDE

You do remember those; don't you?

As if the strangers needed any assistance from the Africans, but to help the strangers begin their enslavement of Africans, slave kingdoms in parts of Africa: Sudan, Congo, Angola, just to name a few, paved the way for slavery as well. These strangers all over the continent began to negotiate with the African fathers, elders, town chiefs, and kinsmen, to allow their children to be carried into the New World. They would promise the parents that their children would be treated well, have a better life, education, and better opportunities. Many of the mothers, who did not feel good about such arrangements that were being made regarding their children, tried to voice out their objections. They did not want their children to leave them, and be carried into some unknown land. Tried as they did, nonetheless, those good, loving and concerned mothers would never succeed, because their good-natured and loving husbands would try to convince them that the children would be fine. They were going to the New World for a better life, and some day, they would return to help improve their communities in Africa.

As many more Europeans, including Portugese and Spanish explorers and traders got

Jaytoe Anthony Tukan, Sr.

TURNING OF THE TIDE

involved, slavery was, without a doubt, out of the hands of African fathers and kinsmen, but into the hands of politicians and rulers in Africa. Selling and buying Africans at slave markets had become a big business between 1600 and 1800 A.D.

Sadly to say, those children would never return to Africa. So many decades would go by, but the parents could not hear from their children. Many mothers and fathers would leave this world, taking that grief for their lost children, into their early graves in Africa.

The children in the New World would grow up, still under slavery, working on plantations, bearing the heat of the sun in hot summers, and suffering in the unbearable cold winters for years, as some would die of pneumonia, other illnesses and diseases. The slaves who survived the horrible weathers would later get married and have children of their own, though conditions for them would not get any better, as there was no sign of relief in sight. For freedom, citizenship, and rights, even for the children who were born in the New World (America at this point), the slaves were always told to forget it; it wasn't going to happen at all.

Don't you still remember way back when the stranger-missionaries had also introduced someone

Jaytoe Anthony Tukan, Sr.

TURNING OF THE TIDE

to the Africans while some of them were still on their continent? The Supreme God of the whole universe? Well, the Supreme God, who knows all things, sees all deeds - good or bad, was still on His Supreme Throne, even over the very New World, compassionately watching the anguish of the slaves. He was not some man-made, absent-minded god, who could not hear, though many of the slaves were asking: "How long, God? How long, before our ordeal is over? God, how long will we suffer?"

It seemed like every time those questions were asked, God would reply, "Hang in there a little while longer, my children."

Then the year 1868 had finally arrived. The 14th Amendment was added to the Constitution of the United States of America. Black people in America were finally granted their citizenship rights. A new day had dawned on the nation. It was truly a brand new day in America.

~~~~~~~~~~~~~~~

Today is a new day in America. America has come a long way. A black man is in the White House today. He is there, not because he's on a school trip, non is he there as a tourist, or a leader

Jaytoe Anthony Tukan, Sr.

TURNING OF THE TIDE

from another country. The African American man is at the White House this time because he is truly the President of these United States of America.

What can be more amazing news to hear? What then must we say at this point? Should we now sing praises and glory for what we see thus far? Surely, we are thankful to God about what's happening in America today. Notwithstanding, does the fact that an African American is the president, erase the wrongs, or the lynches of the past? Are we now prepared to say that "All is well that ends well," in the words of Shakespeare? I wish we could. I truly wish we could all rejoice and say that all is well. No, but all is not well. We all still have a long, long way to go.

Even at this moment, there are agents of hate who lose sleep every night over the fact that a black man is truly the president of the United States. There is a **handwriting** on the wall which spells out change and healing for this nation, but that **handwriting** is still not yet clear to some people. So while healing has truly begun for this nation, while true renewal has truly come to America, these agents of hate, these very uncompromising individuals still have yet to receive the message for America. Today is a day of re-awakening. We are living in a new

Jaytoe Anthony Tukan, Sr.

TURNING OF THE TIDE

America, a nation, so full of hopes, aspirations, and dreams. Today is an important milestone for the world at large. Do you want the rest of the world to move forward without you? Can we count on you, and let us all rebuild America together?

Slavery is inhumane. Slavery creates so much devastation in people's lives. Slavery is selfish. The atrocious conditions that slavery and racism create, are even worse than the human lips will ever be able to describe. Add slavery to racism, and you will hear lynching come knocking at the door. 'I am Mr. Charles Lynch. Got some colored people in there? Hand them over to me, and I will lynch them all for you'all.' This is the result of slavery and racism.

Give me your undivided attention, as I take you back to the very first chapter of this book, where a black boy was presented to be drowning. When his friend, a white boy, tried to rush to his rescue, he was held back. Your humble servant symbolically presented these two friends, and indicated that the white boy was held back. The symbolic holding back of this white boy, was it the action of his parents because they were afraid of what the crowd would think or do? Was this holding back due to racism?

Jaytoe Anthony Tukan, Sr.

TURNING OF THE TIDE

The situation regarding these two friends symbolizes racism and slavery. Back in those days, when a black boy was being hanged, many, many white people motionlessly stood by, and refused to fight to save that boy from dying. Honestly, I am also mindful of the fact that not all the white people who stood by truly favored the lynching of the slaves. On the contrary, some of them saw friends or family members get lynched because they spoke out against such a heinous crime. So those white people, who could have done something to save that black child, or that black man, did nothing. They could have stood up against racism and injustice, but failed to do so for their own safety and the safety of their loved ones.

Can you just imagine yourself being placed in a position like that? You would not fight back, even though you know you have the ability, perhaps the power, to do some good, to save that person from dying, you fail to do so. Yet you keep all that emotion within. What an emotional pain for one to bear. The French Philosopher, Jean-Jacques Rousseau, said it best: "Man is born free, and everywhere he is bound in chains." Those white people, though they had the desire to save a black person in the name of true justice, would not do so,

Jaytoe Anthony Tukan, Sr.

because they, too, were held by fear. They were truly 'bound in chains.'

There were other white people, without a doubt, back in slavery and the civil rights days, who had a heart that bled. Those white people hurt inside, too, like the black people did, when some inhumane act was committed against a black person. Even in America today, I truly believe there are still so many white people, who have a heart that bleeds today when some act of discrimination is committed against a black person, or any other member of a minority group. Let's face it, not all white people were racists back then; needless to say, not all white people are racists today.

I have a few white friends, some of whom have paid my electric bill, making it possible for my apartment to be well-lighted when I was out of the country. Some of my white neighbors have made it their business to question somebody they had not seen around my yard in the past, but claiming to be visiting me when I am not home. These neighbors would demand that the visitor leave, to come back when I am home, or they would call the police on that person. A white man protecting a black man's home? You and I both know that this white guy is different from the racists we have seen around.

Jaytoe Anthony Tukan, Sr.

TURNING OF THE TIDE

For the brave white people who bled to death for sympathizing with black people, they were tired of the heartless acts committed against black people. For them, it was very much incomprehensible that the forefathers of our great nation would actually create a document, which declares, "We hold these truths to be self-evident that all men are created equal," yet others within the same nation decided to treat their fellow citizens unequally. So those white people, like those among the Freedom Riders[3], who were on the right side of justice, chose rather to be lynched with the injustices that took many black people into their early graves.

Memory of grave images continues to flash before the eye of a nation, America, for the blood of all victims of racism. Medgar Evers, leader of the Black Panthers, was a victim, gunned down on June 11, 1963, right at his own doorsteps, as he was returning from work as field secretary for the NAACP in Jackson, Mississippi. Unfortunately, he

---

[3] **Freedom Riders included blacks and whites on buses around the United States, demanding equal rights for all in the 1960s.**

85 **Jaytoe Anthony Tukan, Sr.**

died a few hours later at the hospital.

James Meredith was also a victim, killed as he took on a 'lone demonstration' mission for justice and equality, in Mississippi. James was criticized by some civil rights members, claiming that his mission was 'ill-conceived,' because he did not collaborate within a group. So? Acting alone or not, for him it was still a mission worth taking.

On September 15, 1963, four little black girls: Addie Collins, Carol Robertson, Carol McNair, and Cynthia Wesley, lost their lives, when the Sixteenth Street Baptist Church in Birmingham, Alabama, was bombed by white segregationists. The entire church was set ablaze.

Three civil rights employees were murdered in Philadelphia, Mississippi, on June 21, 1964: James E. Chaney, black, 21; Andrew Goodman, white, 20; and Michael H. Schwerner, white, 24. Eighteen men were arrested by the FBI in October, 1964, for those crimes, but the case never made it to trial for lack of evidence.

In his article, *Justice Overdue*, Borgna Brunner writes, "On January 7, 2005, four decades after the crime, Edgar Ray Killen, then 80, was charged with three counts of murder. Killen was accused of being the mastermind behind the heinous

TURNING OF THE TIDE

crimes. On June 21—the 41st anniversary of the murders, ---Killen was convicted on three counts of manslaughter, a lesser charge." Killen got 60 years in prison.

The blood of these and so many other victims of slavery and racism, continues to cry out from their graves, spreading around America, appealing to all to stop the hatred, to stop the bigotry, and to put an end to racism.

Realistically, I don't believe that racism can ever be wiped out of America. It is like asking people to eradicate poverty, of which I am not even convinced if that is possible. As humans, however, we still have the ability to curtail the problems of racism and poverty, and diminish the effects of the devastation thereof.

President Kennedy addressed the nation on the evening of June 11, 1963, on the issue of race relations. *"One hundred years of delay have passed since President Lincoln freed the slaves; yet their heirs, their grandsons, are not fully free. They are not fully freed from the bonds of injustice. They are not yet freed from* social and *economic oppression, and this nation, for all its hopes and all its boasts, will not be fully free until all its citizens are free."*

Jaytoe Anthony Tukan, Sr.

TURNING OF THE TIDE

President Kennedy ended his statement with a special plea to the U.S. Congress to pass a 'civil rights legislation' as quickly as possible. Of all nights, a few hours after the speech, Mr. Medgar Evers was murdered. Was this in response to the president's message?

Some of us, perhaps many of us today, can not understand in the twenty-first century, why the issue of race and racism still lingers on, and continues to tear us apart, as if each piece of the civil rights laws has done no good, as if too many people have not already lost their lives to racism and slavery. I can not comprehend it today, how America, which is a nation of people helping people, will dwell so much on racism and hatred at this time of our existence as a nation.

Part of the problem we face, I believe, is that we are not open; we refuse to make ourselves available to dialogue often on the issue of race. Racism has become such a sensitive issue that we act like it does not exist, but the reality could not be farther from the truth.

Honestly, we refuse to admit to ourselves that we have a serious problem which needs addressing. How can we ever find a solution, or any resolution,

Jaytoe Anthony Tukan, Sr.

TURNING OF THE TIDE

if we fail to recognize that there is a problem? We behave like we love one another, but deep down within us, there is still that hidden racism, that real bigotry, and concealed animosity, and all of these continue to tear us apart.

We get ourselves ready very quickly to respond to a tragedy in another country; yet we do not care to get to know the name and the needs of our neighbor. It seems like we love to help other people as long as they are not within our 'good' territory. 'Yes, you stay in your country, and let me stay in mine. If you need my help, I will take the next airplane to come and give you all the assistance you need. As for coming to my country, don't even think of it; do not ever come setting foot on my land. For the day you do, that will be the day you will surely see my true color.'

Is this the true America? Is this the America where everybody still wants to come? And when they get here and become our neighbors, they are on their own? If tragedy strikes in their family, their American neighbors will turn the other way?

People outside of America do not ever think that homelessness exists in America. Then they come here, and to their shocking eyes, they see homeless people all in our streets, all over the richest

Jaytoe Anthony Tukan, Sr.

TURNING OF THE TIDE

country in the world. Is it because we do not care for one another? Yet we care for people in a distant land? America, can we put someone up for awhile?

Can we sometimes go back to Los Angeles, California, and heed to the advice of someone? "We are stuck here for a while. Can we get along here?" said Rodney King, the victim himself, in the 1995 LA Police Brutality Case.

America is a nation of nations; we are a country of diversities. We must embrace the good in one another, accept our diversities, rebuild our nation, as we look forward every day to a better tomorrow.

Jaytoe Anthony Tukan, Sr.

Chapter Six

LIFE OF ANN DUNHAM

Stanley Ann Dunham was born on November 29, 1942, in Fort Leavenworth, Kansas. At her birth, she was named after her father, who gave his daughter the 'Stanley' name because he had expected a boy.

Ann's parents, Stanley Dunham and Madelyn Payne, found each other in Wichita, Kansas, and got married on May 5,1940. Ann's heritage is a combination of English, Irish, and German. Thus it is believed she was a distant cousin of two former presidents of the United States: George Bush and Harry Truman, and a former vice president: Dick Cheney. So does that really make Obama somehow a relative of Cheney, who is now very critical of the President?

TURNING OF THE TIDE

Ann's father joined the U. S. Army, after Pearl Harbor, while her mother worked at some Boeing plant in Wichita. At the end of World War II, the family moved around: California, Texas, and Washington State. In 1956, the family left Seattle, and made their way to Mercer Island, Washington, in order for Ann to attend Mercer Island High School.

Because of the unusual way she was named, Ann went through teasing as a child by other children. Some of her high school classmates remembered how things were in the 1960s, a decade which was just beginning when they were graduating.

According to the Chicago Tribune, "Her name was something to tolerate – barely," said Elaine Johnson, the two rode the school bus together.

"I know, it's a boy's name, and no, I don't like it," said Ann to Elaine.

"I mean, would you like to be called Stanley?" Elaine asked.

"But my dad wanted a boy and he got me. And the name 'Stanley' made him feel better, I guess," Ann replied.

Jaytoe Anthony Tukan, Sr.

TURNING OF THE TIDE

"Hers was a mind in full tilt," said Susan Blake, another classmate, who once changed baby Barack's diapers. Susan later became a politician, working as a councilwoman for Mercer Island.

Chip Wall considered Ann "a fellow traveler. If you were concerned about something going wrong in the world, Stanley would know about it first. We were liberals before we knew what liberals were."

"Ann was intellectually way more mature than we were and a little bit ahead of her time, in an off-center way," said another classmate, Jill Burton-Dascher.

About dating and having children which made some of her friends to be baby-sitting their own children so early, Ann did not have any interest at all. Ann felt that she needed to go to school. The Baltimore Sun quoted Maxine Box, Ann's best friend on the topic of dating.

"She felt she didn't need to date or marry or have children. It wasn't a put-down, and it wasn't hurtful. That's just who she was. She was always

Jaytoe Anthony Tukan, Sr.

challenging, arguing, and comparing. She was already thinking about things that the rest of us hadn't."

After they graduated and Ann moved away, Maxine received a letter from her in which Ann mentioned, "Remember me when you are old and gray. Love and luck."

Those were the good old days for the class of 1960 for Mercer Island High School. Didn't we all have them? I still remember my good old days with my high school buddies. Don't you still remember yours?

By the time she got to college, Ann felt that enough was enough; it was time to drop her first name. In 1960, after Ann graduated from high school, the Dunham family made yet another move, this time to Hawaii.

In a Russian language class, at the University of Hawaii at Manoa, there sat an eighteen-year-old girl, who stood out from among all the girls, in the eye of the university's first African student, Obama.

From the Nyanza Province in Kenya, Barack Obama's country had just signed a joint-education agreement with the United States by the time he graduated from high school. He was the very first

TURNING OF THE TIDE

beneficiary to take advantage of the opportunity to attend college in America. The stipulation of the contract was that he would return home after completing college, to serve his country. Obama entered the university in 1959 to study economics.

An outspoken student, Obama spoke on behalf of other students, especially fighting for other foreign students. He was the first president of the International Students Association, of which he was also a founding member. The pair (Barack and Ann) fell in love, and a romantic period followed. About a year later, they tied the knot on February 2, 1961, even though Ann's parents had their reservation. Obama's parents in Africa were also against the idea of an interracial union. Those were the 1960's, a period of intense racial tension in the United States of America; talk about risky days for the couple. But, where there is love, does outside resistence or interference ever work? Do we not hear it from the

 Scriptures that 'Love conquers all'? Sometimes it is necessary for the individuals involved to find out for themselves. This couple surely did, later on, of course.

Barack Hussein Obama, Jr. was born on August 4,1961, at the

Jaytoe Anthony Tukan, Sr.

TURNING OF THE TIDE

Kapi'olani Medical Center in Honolulu, Hawaii. The following summer, his father graduated with honor, receiving a bachelor's degree in economics in June, 1962. Upon graduation, the senior Obama received admissions from New York University and Harvard University at the same time, with both coming with scholarship offers. It is said that New York University's offer would have allowed Obama, Sr. to work and be able to support his young family. However, working while attending college was the farthest thing on his agenda; therefore, he chose to attend Harvard, starting in the fall of 1962.

That summer, the baby, then a year old, and his mother, joined Obama, Sr., in Cambridge. However, it appeared that Ann's plans did not go as well as she had hoped, so she had to leave Massachusetts with her son to return to Hawaii.

Turning down the scholarship from New York University had lessened the senior Obama's ability to support his wife and their young baby. Therefore, it created a strain and much friction on the beautiful young family, as Ann truly felt she was left with no choice, but to file for a divorce in January of 1964, in Honolulu. Surprisingly, the divorce was never ever contested by the baby's father; therefore, it was granted.

Jaytoe Anthony Tukan, Sr.

TURNING OF THE TIDE

After receiving his master's degree in Economics in 1965, Mr. Obama had to return to Kenya in fulfillment of his part of the contract under which his country paid for his education. Probably because of the great distance between the two countries: America and Kenya, coupled with his obligation to serve his country, Mr. Obama did not get to see his son again until six years later. Young Barack was 10 years old in 1971, when his father finally came back to the United States to see him. The feelings of the younger Obama were somewhat mixed. But he suppressed such feelings in order to enjoy what would be the last time he would have with his father.

In this life, there are children who will go on living grudgingly, and would not try to forgive a parent for not being at their very first musical recital, for not being able to carry them to their first basketball game, football game, or for not being around at all. Those children, who carry malice for a lifetime, are the children who miss out on their blessings from God. A forgiving child is always a blessed child.

I believe, however, that many children are very much forgiving when it comes to their biological parents. Whatever the sin that a parent

Jaytoe Anthony Tukan, Sr.

TURNING OF THE TIDE

commits, that sin is usually forgiven. Barack is a blessed child because he did not hesitate to form a bond with his father; he had forgiven him for being an absentee in his life. But there was that month to share with his father. So why not make the best of it and have fun with him?

Barack got on the dance floor with him when his father put on the music from the forty-five records he brought for him in 1971. The following quote is taken from his *Dreams from My Father:* "Come, Barry, you will learn from the master. And suddenly his slender body was swaying back and forth, the lush sound was rising, his arms were swinging as they cast an invisible net, his feet wove over the floor in off-beats..." Barack continued to speak of how exciting it was to see his father on the dance floor:

"I took my first tentative steps with my eyes closed, down, up, my arms swinging, the voices lifting. And I hear him still: as I follow my father into the sound, he lets out a quick shout, bright and high, a shout that leaves much behind and reaches out for more, a shout that cries for laughter."

What an exciting time to have with one's father. You humble servant feels like he was present, and watching the unfolding dancing steps of father and son sway into one direction together, then back

Jaytoe Anthony Tukan, Sr.

TURNING OF THE TIDE

again into the opposite direction. No child would want to miss that with his or her parent.

It is not clear whether or not, father and son ever met again, in the years prior to the death of Barack Obama, Sr. Nevertheless, he met his tragic death in an automobile accident in Kenya in 1982.

During Barack's run for president, the media was very critical of his father, for his choosing Harvard University over the other university. Going to New York University, on the other hand, the media claims, would have enabled him to support his family and keep everyone together. This is a valid point, with which I have no quarrel at all. I understand very well the criticism from the media. He was under an obligation to keep his young family together. Yet, keeping his promise to serve his country was another obligation. How do you keep both commitments?

The beauty of life and the enticing attractions that life itself presents unto us, can sometimes be so overly tempting for some people to resist. Therefore, we must be very mindful in making promises to other people, for a promise is a binding obligation which should be kept. The fact of the matter is, others will see us, want to get to know us, perhaps depend on us, and undoubtedly judge us, based on the promises we make. When we do not keep a

Jaytoe Anthony Tukan, Sr.

TURNING OF THE TIDE

promise, when we decide not to meet an obligation, this shows a serious failure in us to being true to our word. From all honesty, are we only going to be talking the talk, but not also walking the walk? Is that how we want to be perceived?

Here we see the Senior Obama being caught between two worlds. The first is his native land, Kenya, in dire need of educators, and so agreed, and to whom he confidently signed a contract, promising to return home, if that home was to help pay for his college education. The second is the new world, America, within which he created a family, by marriage and the birth of a son, to whom he was then truly obligated. Thus the undeniable question was: which side do I turn?

Turning one way or the other was not really the point, because either way, he was truly breaking a promise, hurting someone, and not being man-up enough to step up to the plate. Truly, since it became impossible for him to keep those two commitments at the same time, Mr. Obama chose to go back home. To put it bluntly, he abandoned his son!

In Africa, Mr. Hussein Obama already had a wife and children before coming to America for college. Definitely, he was supposed to return to that family afterwards. But here was the great sixty-four-million-dollar question which must be answered.

Jaytoe Anthony Tukan, Sr.

TURNING OF THE TIDE

What would really happen if the marriage between him and Barack's mother had survived until it was time for him to return to Africa at the completion of his study? What would he say to his American wife? 'Oh, by the way, Ann, I forgot to mention to you at the beginning of our relationship, that I have another wife in Africa to whom I need to return?' Was it not better for him to allow Ann to end their marriage before it went any further?

I personally do not think Ann would have had any problem with going to live in Kenya with her husband so they both could raise their son together. I also believe that Obama's African wife would have had no problem with her husband bringing home an American wife, or two more wives for that matter, for all of them to live together and be a one big happy family. Nevertheless, the other question was: would Ann, a white American lady, agree to live with a mate, another wife to her husband? Frankly, I do not think so.

During his first visit to Kenya, Barack had a conversation with his grandmother, Mrs. Onyango, the woman he refers to as 'Granny.' In his *Dreams from My Father,* he quotes her:

"What happened in America, I cannot say. I know that after less than two years we received a letter from Barack (your father) saying that he had

Jaytoe Anthony Tukan, Sr.

TURNING OF THE TIDE

met this American girl, Ann, and that he would like to marry her. Now, Barry, you have heard that your grandfather disapproved of this marriage. This is true, but it is not for the reasons you say."

Onyango, the Senior Obama's father did not think his son was doing the right thing. He already had an obligation to his wife and children back home. He then reminded his son in a letter.

"'How can you marry this white woman when you have responsibilities at home? Will this woman return with you and live as a Luo woman? Will she accept that you already have a wife and children? I have not heard of white people understanding such things. Their women are jealous and used to being pampered. But if I am wrong in this matter, let the girl's father come to my hut and discuss the situation properly. For this is the affairs of elders, not children.'

"We are all happy that this marriage took place, because without it we would not have you with us now," Mrs. Onyango concluded.

Choosing between Harvard University and New York University should not require a brain work for any of us, the same way Barack's father did not need to consult a rocket scientist to make that decision. A young man with a strong desire to attend

Jaytoe Anthony Tukan, Sr.

TURNING OF THE TIDE

one of the best universities in the world, Mr. Obama, Sr., truly did not want to settle for any mediocrity in selecting a college for his graduate study.

Africa, comparatively, is no match to America, when it comes to opportunities, be they educational or otherwise. For an African young man to achieve that great academic excellence, making tough choices sometimes becomes a part of the territory. By this statement, I hope I do not appear to be defending the Senior Obama. No, not at all. I am only looking at the situation from another angle, from an African child's point of view, if you would.

For the most part, many, many parents in Africa, though with the strong desire for their children to go to school, can not afford simple school supplies like a pencil which may cost a dime, or a ruler which may cost a quarter. Even if the child is kicked out of school, which is usually the case in many African schools, because of a lack of school supplies as simple as those two mentioned examples, what can the parents do? If a father can not afford to buy these items, it is a tough luck for the child. Nobody, not even the government, non the school, gives out free school supplies in Africa. So a child who is kicked out of school will stay out until at such a time that the need is met. Therefore,

Jaytoe Anthony Tukan, Sr.

TURNING OF THE TIDE

when African children get an opportunity to study abroad, especially in a country called America, many of them do not take that lightly. For many, it is a serious matter; they treat this like it is a matter of life and death. They will truly do everything in their power to get the best education they can, from the best universities in the world. In African countries, getting an education, even from public schools, is really never, never free.

In my personal situation in Liberia, my 4th grade teacher at the Assemblies of God Mission School (AGMS), Robert Giplay, told me on a Friday evening as we were leaving class, that I shouldn't go back to school on the following Monday without the ruler, which was required for my math class. My father could not afford the thirty cents for the ruler. Cousin Jonah, who was sharing the apartment with us, was the only person working in a family of five. He had just received his pay, and after paying the rent for that month, the balance was barely enough for us to buy food until the end of another two weeks. So that meant I would miss school for two weeks because of a ruler. Did my father not truly have a strong desire to keep his kid in school? Of course he did. Strong desire or not, so what? He just did not have the extra thirty cents for the ruler.

Jaytoe Anthony Tukan, Sr.

TURNING OF THE TIDE

Taking that amount from the food money of fifty cents per day, would mean the whole family of five going without food for a day. Giving the reverse, would you, dear reader, not have chosen rather to put food on the table for your family, than buying a ruler for your child to go to school?

I did not want to miss school for two weeks; it was a long time for a child to stay away. Therefore, I did the most unthinkable thing a child my age would do. Without the knowledge of my parents, I went out on the following Monday morning, standing on the sidewalk, looking for work for a day.

Fortunately for me, a pickup truck came by, loaded with bags of cement and a group of boys. The driver needed one more boy; so I jumped on board. We worked all day, loading and unloading cement bags from 8:00-4:00 on that sunny Monday. After receiving my pay of $1.00 for the day, I was able to buy the ruler, and still had change left over to give to my mother to help put food on the table for another day. From the balance 70 cents, my mother gave 30 cents to another mother whose struggling family of six was living on 30 cents per day. Boy! And here was I thinking we had it bad. But there was a family of six next door.

Jaytoe Anthony Tukan, Sr.

TURNING OF THE TIDE

Up until I graduated from college, my father did not know the truth about how that ruler was bought. It was a secret between my mother and me. I would truly have gotten a whipping from my father for going out there and working when I was underage. Yes, he was truly going to punish me for helping him out with his obligation. Imagine that.

I hope, with the above example, you can now really understand the situation that other children, outside of America, go through just to obtain an education, which in many cases, is free in America. Therefore, when African children get an opportunity to study abroad, especially in a country, called America, many of them do not waste time, particularly if they know that their financial support is coming from the pocket of someone other than their parents. They take their education seriously. When it comes to education in Africa, there's only "one life to live."

Now let's get back on track here. In this case, however, the Senior Obama erred very greatly by turning his back on his young family. But, didn't life go on with Ann and her child? Disappointed she was to see her marriage end so soon, but Ann did not roll over on her back, gazing up in the sky, and hoping for manna to fall from heaven. She had to continue

Jaytoe Anthony Tukan, Sr.

TURNING OF THE TIDE

to press on, as she raised her baby without his father.

Sometimes a situation like this can be a great motivator for some individuals to reach for the stars. We do see her strong will to succeed, "a determination to continue, regardless the obstacles,"[4] which Ann had turned into one of her many great challenges of life she decided to face headstrong. She, without any hesitation, re-enrolled at the University of Hawaii. This perseverance paid off on August 6, 1967, two days after Barack's 6th birthday, when she graduated with a bachelor of arts in mathematics. That same year, we would see Ann getting married to another International student, Lolo Soetoro, an Indonesian. Perhaps this was Ann's graduation present. The new family later moved to Jakarta, where Barack spent some of his early school years. From this new union, a new baby came, Maya Kassandra Soetoro, born on August 15, 1970.

Ann, a resilient woman, turned many obstacles into great challenges. Giving birth to a son at age 19, being left a single mother at age 20, she never gave up, no, not at all. Ann was never a quitter. Getting married again at age 25 in 1967,

---

[4] Dr. James Pula, in his Foreword to The Other End Of The Tunnel, 1998.

Jaytoe Anthony Tukan, Sr.

TURNING OF THE TIDE

separating from her second husband at age 30 in 1972, thus becoming a single mother again, but this time, of two children: Barack and Maya, Ann still found the way to bounce back, making life worth living.

Yes, there were many crooked bridges she felt she needed to tear down, and many more solid bridges to build. We would see her again in 1974, as she returned to college. Juggling between her schooling in America and her job as a weaver in Indonesia, while at the same time ending her second marriage in 1980, Ann still found the way to earn her graduate degree on December 18, 1983, in anthropology from the same university. Her dream to further her education still remained in tack.

Ann went back to the University of Hawaii to work on her doctorate, under the supervision of Professor Alice Dewey. At the end, she wrote a dissertation: Peasant Blacksmithing in Indonesia: surviving and thriving against all odds. Almost 50 years old, Ann, on August 9, 1992, finally received her Ph.D. in anthropology. Personally, I think the sub-title of Ann's dissertation, *surviving and thriving against all odds*, describes her very well. From all reality, Ann was a survivor and a lady who thrived against all odds; she continued to bounce

Jaytoe Anthony Tukan, Sr.

TURNING OF THE TIDE

back over and over again. Ann finally moved back to Hawaii to live near her mother.

At age 52, Ann lost her battle to ovarian cancer in 1995.

Looking back at what we know about Barack's parents, do we still wonder about his strength and unwavering character, and from where he gets such qualities or characteristics? It is obvious he gets those from both his father and mother. They did not possess the quitting spirit. Rather, they were resilient individuals who valued life and knew how to diligently prepare for it.

Jaytoe Anthony Tukan, Sr.

Up until I graduated from college, my father did not know the truth about how that ruler was bought. It was a secret between my mother and me. I would truly have gotten a whipping from my father for going out there and working when I was underage. Yes, he was truly going to punish me for helping him out with his obligation. Imagine that.

Chapter Seven

SURPRISES IN KENYA

There is one thing all Americans and other foreigners must know about Africa when setting foot on the continent: the rules, as you know them in the western world, do not apply in Africa. At the street corner, in the marketplace, workplace, or airport, the rules are never the same; they change all the time, depending on where you are, and with whom you are dealing. I can not place any more emphasis on this enough; just remember: rules in Africa are never consistent.

First of all, Obama arrives at Kenyatta International Airport. All other passengers get their bags; he does not get his. A security officer approaches him, asks him for a cigarette, and he gives the officer one. Barack inquires of the officer if all the unloading from the airplane was done, and the officer says yes. In the process of their short

Jaytoe Anthony Tukan, Sr.

TURNING OF THE TIDE

conversation, the officer finds out Obama is an American, which is a good thing, a blessing, in a way, not for Obama, but for the officer. Obama makes his first mistake after the officer offers his help by getting an airline worker for him to talk about his missing luggage. He does not give the officer a "tip" (a small change) for assisting him. Giving a "tip" in Africa to get things done is a normal way of life; it is not a crime.

Next the British Airways worker, Miss Omoro, discovers from the filled-out form by Barack, that he is the American son of Dr. Barack Obama, Sr., who, though deceased and gone, is still very popular in Kenya.

Again, because he is not familiar with the system in Africa, he fails to give this woman a "tip" when he is expected to do so. For all intended purposes, his bags could have been right there at the airport. He does not know that he needs to tip these people in order to expedite his search for the missing luggage (if those items were missing at all); so he misses out. Hello? Is anybody listening?

Am I passing judgment on Barack here? Not at all, far from it. I am only assuming, based on my reading his *Dreams from My Father,* either he tipped the workers at the airport and chose that his act of

Jaytoe Anthony Tukan, Sr.

TURNING OF THE TIDE

kindness should not be mentioned, or he just simply did not offer any tips, which kind gesture was still in his power to do or not to do. However, my message to Americans and other travelers to the continent of Africa, is a lesson that I hope they will keep in mind. I am still of the assumption that no tips were given during his airport dilemma.

Two days later, when his luggage did not arrive, Obama's sister, Auma, took him back to the airport to inquire about those items. Surprisingly, they were told that there was no record of him ever filling out a form for any missing bags. He asked to speak to Miss Omoro, who previously took the filled-out form from him; they were told that the lady was on vacation. Here again, he made the very same mistake for the third time by not tipping these people. He only thought that by speaking to these workers with an empty-mouth, he would really get anywhere with them.

Their next encounter was dealing with the clerk at the downtown head office of the British Airways. She, for some reason, or for no apparent reason at all, was angry with the pair; she left their presence, got behind the window, closed the window, and became absent-minded. Her refusal to have anything to do with the couple was a clear

Jaytoe Anthony Tukan, Sr.

TURNING OF THE TIDE

handwriting on the wall, which Auma, who is more a Kenyan than her brother is, should have seen and read very clearly. This latest incident was a very good indicator that you should not hold tight to your money if you want to get things done in Africa. You don't get anywhere in Africa for a missing bag or anything like that, by not giving the people some money, if I can spell it out to you all. Money, money, money, is the nature of the game, if you need to do business in Africa. Is anybody home?

And people say 'what you don't know does not ever hurt you?' Well, if President Obama ever believed this statement, he probably might want to rethink his belief, after reading my advice. Trust me, what you don't know, my friend, really, really hurts you. There is no beating around-the-bush about this.

The size of the African family tree is very large. It begins with the patriarchs, down to the children, grandchildren, and extends all the way to nephews, nieces, uncles, aunties, cousins, and many other members who are not blood-relatives. Some of your acquaintances and friends are also included in this extended African family circle.

Many westerners, some of whom might have lived in Africa for a short period, may think they know Africa and its people. But the simple reality,

Jaytoe Anthony Tukan, Sr.

TURNING OF THE TIDE

my dear, is that strangers may never truly, and truly understand the nature of the African family. While many, a stranger, may only imagine the African family and wonder while Africans cater to outsiders who are not even related to them by blood, Africans, themselves live this life; so they understand very well the structure of the African family. They can attest to the fact that the responsibility of a large family like the Obamas, can be borne by a single family member like Auma, and the effect can be very overwhelming, though many Africans do not ever consider this a burden.

Going back home. I know that every culture is different and unique to its own people, and there is also much excitement when someone returns home from a long trip, or from a very faraway country. It can be a great occasion.

For the African child, going back home is more than a great occasion; it is a joyous and endless season. For someone like me who grew up not even a teenager, before Moses, my elder brother, took me away from our village to Monrovia, the Capital City of Liberia, about a thousand miles away, going back home was such an endless season of great jubilation and celebration.

Jaytoe Anthony Tukan, Sr.

TURNING OF THE TIDE

I was a third grader when Moses took me away, but he was taking me back to our village a teenager and a high school graduate. This was during the Christmas Season. That made it that much more fun. What a great season of celebration for the entire village it was. It was such a big deal not only for my family, but for the whole village, also because I was the very first child from our town to finish high school. Moses, after completing junior high school, unselfishly put his life and schooling on hold, worked two jobs to put me through school till my graduation from high school. Can you imagine that? Moses should have been the first high school graduate from our town, but he gave up that honor for me. This unselfish nature in my big brother also made it such a big deal for the entire village. The celebration could not end, starting in mid December to the end of January.

Even if the child was born outside of his village, like Barack, who was not born in Kenya, it is still a big deal when he finally goes home to that village. Home is still that sweet home for the child, and for the many relatives who have heard so many good things about him before really meeting him. It is truly an occasion of endless season of celebration

Jaytoe Anthony Tukan, Sr.

TURNING OF THE TIDE

for everyone. I believe Barack saw and felt the warm reception he got from everybody.

Intermingling with family members, including those siblings you did not know you had, though surprising it may be, but can be that much more fun. Never mind that someone outside your family circle would very well mistaken you for a deceased family member[5] you had never even met.

Elder brother, Barry, during his visit, and while he interacted with many of his relatives, decided to go one-on-one with his younger brother, Bernard, on the basketball court. What a joy it was for both brothers, but even more especially for Bernard. As the two left the court, Bernard was so excitedly relieved that his big brother, the lost family member, had finally gone home to them. Putting his arm over his big brother's shoulder, Bernard happily said to Barry, "It's good to have a big brother around."

---

[5]

An acquaintance of the family has mistaken Barack to be David, who is deceased. Barack never met David, his brother, (Dreams from My Father, 2005, page 338 Barack Obama).

Jaytoe Anthony Tukan, Sr.

TURNING OF THE TIDE

Going back home, however, may be a little riskier than meets the eye. There are other people who may be completely out of the family circle. In other words, they are not family; definitely, there is no understanding either by family association or by blood, with any of your family members. But my dear, beware!

Yes, they know your parents and your parents know them very well. But that's all there is to it. Let them, notwithstanding, hear the news of your going back home; they will get themselves ready to come out with the wildest relationship stories ever told.

"You know, it's funny how a little baby like you grew up so fast," some of them will begin their narration. "It seems just like yesterday when I held you in my arms, lifting you way up in the air. But thank God you are a big boy now. What did you bring for
me?"

Another sitting nearby, perhaps a lady, replying, "Don't worry; I am the aunty, and you are the uncle. Our son has brought something good for us." Even if you know these two are not family members, still, you better, better find something for them, no matter how little or insignificant you think

Jaytoe Anthony Tukan, Sr.

TURNING OF THE TIDE

that little item may be. Do not ever create unnecessary enemies for yourself and your family members.

"My son! My son! You've been gone for so long," a lady I did not know, began her amazing relationship story when everyone came to celebrate with me during my high school graduation party. She continued,

"Don't you know how your mother and I have grieved so much and so long for you? I hope you brought something good for your mom and me."

"Mom, who was that woman?" I asked Bessie, my mom, after the lady retired to her own house for the evening.

"She's not family. To be honest with you, she is just a woman who thinks she's related to everyone in this town."

"Then we don't have to worry about getting her something; or do we?" I asked my mother again.

"That's where you are wrong, my son. She is a woman not to be reckoned with; we will find a gift for her. You don't want her to truly turn into our lifetime enemy," mother gave me a serious warning. We had to find something for that woman. But home is still a sweet home!

Jaytoe Anthony Tukan, Sr.

TURNING OF THE TIDE

The very first time Barack entered his sister's apartment, he saw a big poster of a black woman hanging on the wall over her bed, which read: "I have a Dream."

"So what's your dream, Auma?" He asked his sister.

Laughing, she said, "That's my biggest problem, Barack. Too many dreams. A woman with dreams always has problems."

Several days later, a conversation between the siblings led them back to that question.

"You wouldn't believe how much I missed Kenya when I was in Germany," Auma began to pour her heart out to her brother. "All I could do was think about getting back home. I thought how I never feel lonely here, and family is everywhere, nobody sends their parents to an old people's home or leaves their children with strangers. Then I'm here and everyone is asking me for help, and I feel like they are all just grabbing at me and that I'm going to sink. .... But what can I do, Barack? I'm only one person."

Barack took his sister's hand into his palm, consoling her as they both sat in the car, watching the rain pour very, very heavily.

Jaytoe Anthony Tukan, Sr.

TURNING OF THE TIDE

"You asked me what my dream was," the sister continued. "Sometimes I have this dream that I will build a beautiful house on our grandfather's land. A big house where we can all stay and bring our families, you see. We could plant fruit trees like our grandfather, and our children would really know the land and speak Luo and our ways from the old people. It would belong to them."

"We can do all that, Auma," Barack told his sister.

Jumping back in, Auma said, ..."Now I'm used to living my own life, just like a German.Everything is organized. If something is broken, I fix it.... If I have it, I send money to the family, and they can do with it what they want, and I won't depend on them, and they won't depend on me."

"It sounds lonely," Barack told his big sister, who seemed a little out of it at this point.

"Oh, I know, Barack. That's why I keep coming home. That's why I'm still dreaming."

I hope the President of the United States, who is also Auma Obama's younger brother, remembers

Jaytoe Anthony Tukan, Sr.

TURNING OF THE TIDE

this conversation. I do also hope that Barack, most importantly, still remembers his response to his sister: "We can do all that, Auma."

So I ask you, Mr. President, have you helped Auma to build that big, beautiful house yet? If you did, I extend my personal thanks to you. If not, then the time to build is in fact overdue. Let's build now!

Chapter Eight

COMMUNITY ORGANIZER?

After graduating from Punahou School in 1979, Obama enrolled at Occidental College in Los Angeles, California, to work on his Associates degree. After a while, he matriculated to Columbia University in New York (1981). In 1983, Obama completed his bachelor's degree, graduating in Political Science.

For a career, Barack Obama wanted to be a community organizer, though he had no idea what the functions of a community organizer were, nor was he able to find a job in his chosen interest. Meanwhile, he accepted a position at the Business International Corporation as a research assistant, and the New York Public Interest Research Group. But his interest in community organizing had not in any

Jaytoe Anthony Tukan, Sr.

TURNING OF THE TIDE

way dissipated, as he continued to talk to co-workers and friends about this. Some of them were skeptical about his choice of a career, but wouldn't express their honest views to him. Only Ike, the security guard in the building where he worked, decided to talk about it.

"Organizing? That's some kinda politics, ain't it? Why you wanna do something like that?" Ike asked Barack. Though he did not really know what a person in that position would do, he tried to tell Ike about wanting to mobilize and help people.

Ike replied,.."Forget about this organizing business and do something that's gonna make you some money.. young man like you, got a nice voice – hell, you could be them announcers on TV. Or sales... Don't waste your youth, Mr. Barack. Wake up one morning, an old man like me, and all you gonna be is tired, with nothing to show for it."

Broadcasting or sales were good careers for a young man with a good voice to consider, not some organizing and mobilizing business, but Barack's interest was not in any of these areas. Neither did he ever get discouraged about not getting positive comments from people about what he really wanted to do. He was still going to be of the mind-set that

Jaytoe Anthony Tukan, Sr.

TURNING OF THE TIDE

some day he would be a community organizer.

After four years in New York, Barack moved to Chicago, and started working as director of the Developing Communities Project (DCP). The organization consisted of eight parishes. During his three years (1985-1988) as director of DCP, the one-person office grew to thirteen; the institution saw its annual budget of $70,000 grow to $400,000. DCP's great accomplishments under Barack included: a tenants' rights organization, a tutoring program, a job training program, to name but a few. At the same time, Barack worked as a teacher and consultant at the Gamaliel Foundation.

During his presidential run, candidate Obama was heavily criticized about his lack of experience. However, one can not help, but notice the areas of involvement, where he truly directed his attention as a place of employment. It did appear from the get-go, that the young man might have really known what he wanted to do; or we might as well go on record in saying, what he was born to do: serve people. Barack believed in a better America, where people's lives could be better, if someone would see the need and help to make a difference for them. Therefore, he obtained assistance from government

Jaytoe Anthony Tukan, Sr.

TURNING OF THE TIDE

and many other sources (churches, for example) to help raise the standard of living for others.

Obama echoed this belief in his speech at the 2004 Convention as he made an appeal to Americans 'to find unity in diversity.' "There is not a liberal America and a conservative America; there's the United States of America."

In 1988, Obama decided to go back to school. He was then admitted to Harvard Law School. At the end of his first year, he became editor of the Harvard Law Review.

During his sophomore year, Barack, at 29, got elected president of the Harvard Law Review. With this opportunity, he became the very first black student to occupy such a position, in which he would supervise eighty editors, working voluntarily as editor-in-chief.

While still in college, Barack Obama continued to go back to Chicago during his summer breaks, and worked as an intern at the law firms of Sidley & Austin in 1989, and Hopkins & Sutter in 1990. After graduating from Harvard University with a law degree in 1991, he decided to settle permanently in Chicago.

Being the first black president of the Harvard

TURNING OF THE TIDE

Law Review created so much attention from the media, paving the way for Barack to receive a contract to write on race relations. The result would later be: *Dreams from My Father.* He worked at several law firms, like Davis, Miner, Barnhill & Galland, practicing as a civil rights lawyer. Here again, this young man could have chosen to remain a civil rights lawyer; or for that matter, he could have retained his position as a constitutional law professor at the University of Chicago. But public service was more important to him than being a law professor, though this was an opportunity to make some big bucks.

Barack returned to what he loves most: serving, energizing, and mobilizing people. He got involved with Illinois' Project Vote in April, 1992. Out of the 400,000 unregistered African-Americans in Illinois, 150,000 were registered by the organization during the period of his involvement.

Obama ran for state senator and won. He was re-elected twice, serving three terms (1997- 2004). In 2000, he ran for a seat in the United States House of Representatives, but did not win. Nevertheless, he did not allow this defeat to make him keep his head

Jaytoe Anthony Tukan, Sr.

TURNING OF THE TIDE

down; it seems it energized him more to keep his head up, and continue looking ahead.

In January 2003, he declared himself a candidate for the U.S. Senate. Jack Ryan became Obama's rival, a very strong opponent from the Republican Party. However, as both campaigns forged on into mid 2003, opinion polls in Illinois favored candidate Obama, putting him far ahead with 53% to 30%. To make matters worse for Jack, the media leaked a sex scandal about his relationship with ex-wife, actress Jeri Ryan. The couple's divorce records, of which both mutually agreed to remain a private matter, were released to the public, and seriously posed a damaging effect on his candidacy. Disappointingly to his constituents, Mr. Ryan withdrew himself from the race in June of 2004, with only four months left before the senatorial election.

Ryan's eventual withdrawal created a vacuum for a Republican to fill. Losing no time to take on the challenge was Alan Keyes, then resident of Maryland, who decided to step up to the plate. Mr. Keyes relocated to Chicago to contend for the seat. However, he lost the election with 27 percent of the vote, as Obama won by 70 percent.

Jaytoe Anthony Tukan, Sr.

TURNING OF THE TIDE

Michelle LaVaughn Robinson was born on January 17, 1964 in Chicago, Illinois, unto Fraser and Marian Robinson. She and elder brother, Craig, were raised by their parents at the family's one-bedroom apartment in Chicago. Their parents were a hard-working family, and became good members of the community. Mr. Robinson, a city pump operator, was very involved with the Democratic process as a precinct captain. But Michelle's father passed away in 1991, possibly from multiple sclerosis.

Craig, Michelle's older brother, was born on April 21, 1962, in Chicago, about two years before Michelle was born. Both children were excellent students, who took very challenging courses. The siblings are both graduates of Princeton University. Craig received his bachelor's degree in Sociology in 1983. While he was still at Princeton, Craig was a star basketball player for the university from 1981-1983.

Craig obtained his MBA from the University of Chicago Graduate School of Business in 1992, majoring in finance. Currently, he works as the Head Basketball Coach at Oregon State University.

Jaytoe Anthony Tukan, Sr.

TURNING OF THE TIDE

Following into big brother Craig's footsteps, Michelle also graduated with honors with a degree in Sociology in 1985. She would later matriculate to Harvard University, from where she earned her law degree in 1988.

Michelle was already working at the law firm of Sidley and Austin as a corporate attorney in 1989 when Barack was hired to work there as an intern. She was his mentor. The first time she heard her would- be husband's name, she wondered about such a funny name. So surprised that she even remarked, "What kinda parents would name their child Barack Obama?" But little did she know that such a funny name would be attached to her name forever. It was during their working together at the law firm that he asked her on a date, which Michelle had initially refused to accept, but finally gave in as he persisted. A courtship followed, as he pursued her, eventually winning her heart to marry him. They got married on October 3, 1992 at the Trinity Church in Chicago. Marrying the couple up was their Pastor, Jeremiah Wright. Barack and Michelle have two daughters: Malia and Sasha.

Later, Michelle became an assistant to Chicago Mayor Richard Daly. In 1993, Mrs. Obama

Jaytoe Anthony Tukan, Sr.

TURNING OF THE TIDE

founded Public Allies Chicago, a non-profit organization, geared towards helping young adults learn leadership skills for public service careers. After a few years, she went to work at the University of Chicago as an associate dean of students in 1996.

In 2005, Michelle was appointed Vice President of Community & External Affairs at the University of Chicago Medical Center. She held this position until January 9, 2009, when she resigned to become the very first black First Lady of the United States.

Jaytoe Anthony Tukan, Sr.

The Newly Wed: October 3, 1992

Chapter Nine

ROAD TO THE OVAL OFFICE

Standing before the nation at the Democratic National Convention in July, 2004, held in Boston, Massachusetts, was an unknown speaker, somebody with a funny name, Barack Obama. Senator John Kerry from Massachusetts, the Party's Nominee, had chosen him to deliver the keynote address that evening. Barack Obama? What kinda name is that? That was the question many people were asking, as the young man stepped up unto the podium. Though he was the three-time state senator from Illinois, and was at this time running for the United State Senate, Barack was still not really known outside of his own state. Since that vibrant

Jaytoe Anthony Tukan, Sr.

TURNING OF THE TIDE

speech, the nation, together with the rest of the world, began to know him and follow his steps, not in the manner of the police or the FBI tailing a criminal; rather, everyone really began to pay close attention to this fellow from Chicago.

From our residence, as my wife and I watched him deliver the keynote address, I had something to say to her. "Honey, if any black person will be president in America some day, this guy will be the first black president."

My wife, somewhat agreed, but indicated that "America still has a long way to go before that will happen." This very statement had always generally been the response from people; there was no doubt about that. Therefore, my dear Niecy did not get any argument from me on that one. We both knew, or so we thought, that this nation would not make it a reality any time soon. However, four years after Senator John Kerry's nomination by the Party, the very young man with the funny name, Barack Hussein Obama, was overwhelmingly elected president of the United States of America on November 4, 2008. Who could ever have thought that this would happen in such a short period of time?

Jaytoe Anthony Tukan, Sr.

TURNING OF THE TIDE

When the U.S. Senator from Illinois announced his bid for the Oval Office on February 10, 2007, I ruled him out; I did not think he would get anywhere. Can you really believe me? Even though in 2004, I felt very strongly that Barack would become the first black president, should he run, I still had doubt that this nation, the United States of America, was truly ready for a black president. It is not that I doubted his ability to mobilize citizens from the bottom up, as he tried to reach everybody: black, white, yellow, no matter the race or origin; I felt, however, it was still a little too early for a black person. In my mind, it was a battle already lost by him before it began.

Why wouldn't I think this way? Why would anybody in America think it was possible for Obama to win? Hadn't Rev. Jessie Jackson twice been there, and done that, in 1984 & 1988, respectively? Had Rev. Alfred Charles Sharpton not been there, and also done that in 2004? Didn't we all see Alan Keyes recently travel the same road, but in vain?

What about Shirley Chisholm? She started all of this. She served in the New York General Assembly from 1964-1968, then ran for U.S. Congress in 1968. She won and became the first

TURNING OF THE TIDE

black woman to serve in Congress. She was re-elected in 1970 to a second term. After serving in Congress, Shirley opened the door to presidential politics for black people in America.

On January 25, 1972, Mrs. Chisholm told fellow citizens, "I stand before you today as a candidate for the Democratic nomination for the Presidency of the United States. I am not the candidate of black America, although I am black and proud. I am not the candidate of the women's movement of this country, although I am a woman, and I am equally proud of that. I am not the candidate of any political bosses or special interests. I am the candidate of the people."

All these black people - had been there and done that, but with no success. Why should any other black person, man or woman, be any different? To me, the Oval Office was the White House, not the Black House. But little did I know that Election Year 2008 was unusually going to be different.

Year 2008 was one of history in the making; it was an election year like none other, that America had ever seen. Never in the history of this country, had Americans seen two minority front-runners, running neck-to-neck with each other, almost all the

TURNING OF THE TIDE

way to the end of a primary. America is a nation, whose history is so intriguing, daring, and very crazy. It appeared that these crazy Americans were again going to the polls to do what is constitutionally done every four years, but this time, they were going to do it differently; they would change presidential politics in the nation forever. Some citizens were about to make the craziest decision of their lives: putting a black man into the White House.

Yes, this was a new nation, absolutely different from the America of yesteryears. A new era was about to dawn on the land, called America. A new chapter was being added to the American story, giving this nation a new phase that would change the history of the United States of America forever, making it more enriching, yet, more astonishing, indeed. This was history in the making! Wasn't it good for America and the world at large? America, you have earned a Big Star! You have earned another Great Stripe!

If ever there was any intense and great competition and rivalry among presidential candidates, the 2008 primary campaigns had produced so much rivalry, along with surprises on

Jaytoe Anthony Tukan, Sr.

TURNING OF THE TIDE

both sides. As is usually the case, the presidential bid starts with many, many candidates, Republicans and Democrats, and sometimes Independents, going at it again, as each in his or her own right, tries to show strength, power, and dignity, as they all must campaign very hard to get a vote. They must compete until suddenly, we see a dwindling in the numbers, as those 'who can not stand the heat must stay out of the kitchen.' Yes, buddy, either you're in, or step aside and let the brave move.

For some of us who love surprises, real surprises were fed to us in 2008. The Senator of New York, Hillary Rodham Clinton, the only female candidate, and wife of former United States President, William Jefferson Clinton, had been the front-runner among the Democrats until the Iowa Caucuses. Very surprisingly, Clinton fell to third place with 29% of the total precincts of 1,781 reporting on Thursday, January 3, 2008. U.S. Senator from Illinois, Barack Hussein Obama, Jr., the only African-American candidate, took the lead, with 38%, as former North Carolina Senator, John Edwards, not too far behind, with 30%.

For the Republicans, Mike Hukabee, a Baptist minister, took the lead with 33% at the end of the Iowa Caucuses, with former Massachusetts governor, Mitt Romney, coming second, 29%, as

Jaytoe Anthony Tukan, Sr.

TURNING OF THE TIDE

Arizona Senator John McCain fell to distant third, 17%. The results in New Hampshire would, nonetheless, be different, as the candidates continued on those long campaign trails. Senator Obama's lead from Iowa would be short-lived, as Senator Clinton took back her lead, winning New Hampshire with 39%, and Obama coming second, 37%, only for the nation to see John Edwards completely out of the race, as he fell to a distant third, 17%.

Speaking about history being made in America today, your humble servant got on the road, as he began to engage in a dialogue with the general public, during which time he posed a question: "What is history?"

Some Americans replied, "History is current events."

Following up, he asked: "What if the events are not current, do we forget the events simply because they are now in the past?"

Some respondents then changed their minds, and indicated that "history is past, current, and future events."

Ah ha! That raises the most important question of the conversation. I then asked again. "Future events? Can we ever truly predict history before it happens?"

Jaytoe Anthony Tukan, Sr.

TURNING OF THE TIDE

So, as you can see, dear reader, that simple question about the definition or the meaning of history generated into a few, but varying answers, calling again for confusion; this shows once more, not so much any ignorance on their part, but the craziness of some Americans.

Could America have ever predicted on August 26, 1920, the day women in this country were "granted their rights to vote and to hold public office," that a woman would be a contestant for the Oval Office, not to even mention, a front-runner like Mrs. Clinton was in 2008? Could the male generation of this country imagine for the future, putting aside all male dominance, that a woman would run for any seat in Congress? In way-back years, could anyone in America ever think that black people would, in generations yet unborn, be among United States presidential candidates? A black man winning his party primary caucuses? Is this history that was future events? Did everyone miss that? The whole nation might have missed that prediction, but a few individuals knew that this day would come.

Rosa Parks was one of them. She refused to 'stand up' or get off the bus in order to preserve whatever little dignity that was left in her, after so many years of injustice, discrimination, intense racism, and inhumane acts against black people.

Jaytoe Anthony Tukan, Sr.

TURNING OF THE TIDE

Rosa's refusal did usher into prominence another individual.

For this reason, a new baby boy from Atlanta, Georgia, would grow up later to see the bondage and atrocities of his people. Like baby Moses, an Israelis child found on the Nile River, who grew up to see the suffering and atrocities in Egypt, and refused all royalty accorded to him for the freedom of his people, this child from Georgia would somehow become the Moses for America. Later, he would show America - the 'evil America', to see her wrongs, injustices, and inequalities, and try to turn herself away from those evils, making them into something more positive.

As Moses was sent out of Egypt, exiled into another land in order for God to prepare him for the great task ahead, 26-year old Martin was sent into harm's way from Georgia to another state, Alabama, as God would also prepare him for the great task ahead.

Thirty-four years after his birth, tired and weary of conditions in America, and standing firmly on the Washington Monument grounds, entirely surrounded by thousands and thousands of fellow citizens, waiting to hear the call for justice in America, Dr. Martin Luther King, Jr., would tell his country in 1963: "I have a dream that one day ......"

141   **Jaytoe Anthony Tukan, Sr.**

TURNING OF THE TIDE

For the sake of his people, Moses did not live long enough to reach the great Promised Land for Israel. God, having sent him to the top of Mount Nebo to get a good view of the Promised Land, would take Moses home to rest.

For the sake of his people, justice and equality in America, Martin did not live long enough to see the freedom of his people, and to see Obama elected President of the United States of America. But he noted: "I've been to the mountaintop.... I just want to do God's will. And He's allowed me to go up to the mountain. And I've looked over. And I've seen the promised land. I may not get there with you. But I want you to know tonight, that we, as a people, will get to the promised land!......"

God would also take Martin home to rest. But the deeds that both men (Moses and Martin) left behind are very much on our lips today.

~~~~~~~~

How much experience can be enough experience to run for the Oval Office? How much experience does one need in order to be the president of the United States of America? How about just being a good public servant? Could this

Jaytoe Anthony Tukan, Sr.

TURNING OF THE TIDE

be one of the criteria? How about mobilizing people, energizing them to believe again? What about helping fellow citizens believe in themselves, that in these United States, our tomorrow can always be better than our today if only we can patiently endue? That out of many, we can all continue to build on this 'One nation, under God, indivisible, with liberty, and justice for all?' Would this not be the 'change' Obama talked about during his campaign?

Did I already mention that, prior to his election to the presidency, Barack Obama achieved his dream of wanting to, some day, become a true community organizer? Possibilities do exist in America, if only you truly believe you can make it. Believing is just one aspect of success; doing what needs to be done in order to achieve success is another. Prepare!

Three presidential debates were held. In all three, before America sat two public servants: one, a soldier, a great military hero with valor of honor, and the other, a Chicago community organizer, a lawyer. But what America saw, most importantly, was a man, very cool, collective, and confident, a man, who did not lose his cool, even when his frustrated rival made an unnecessary attack on him. What the citizens saw was a person, a leader, who

Jaytoe Anthony Tukan, Sr.

TURNING OF THE TIDE

would not rush to judgment in declaring war on another nation, without getting all facts in place. What Americans saw was a leader, who would always make room for diplomacy to play out, unless his back was truly pushed against the wall; then and only then, would he be justified to urging our nation into war.

What this nation needed was a leader who would not be so egotistical so as to urging our soldiers to war in order to show our military might. What this nation longed for, or truly needed, was a leader who would be calm in the midst of crisis, so that he wouldn't rush to making any decision which would be counter-productive. The president of the United States is the leader of the free world, and as such, his decision affects the whole world. We needed someone who would be calm even to the point of responding with a 'smile' when his opponent refers to him as, "that one!" Unbelievable.

We needed a leader who would not only unite races of people into this One Nation which we call America, but will place our nation on the world map as a leader for the free world once again. This was the person the citizens saw in Barack Obama; this was the person Americans got to know in Obama as he campaigned for almost two years, leading up to the general elections of 2008.

144   **Jaytoe Anthony Tukan, Sr.**

TURNING OF THE TIDE

Tuesday, November 4, 2008 had finally arrived; there was no turning back. Citizens went to the polls, as all world citizens watched, with great anticipation to see what would go down. What really went down is that Barack Hussein Obama, the young man from Hawaii, the United States Senator from Illinois, won the 2008 United States Presidential Election by 53 percent of the vote, compared to John McCain, the Republican opponent, who received 46 percent of the vote. The result for North Carolina was not available that night; it came in about two weeks later. Obama won its 15 electoral votes, which he did not need.

How much experience does one need in order to be the President of the United States of America? Well, you do not really have to take my word for it. On November 4, 2008, American citizens already answered that question.

Jaytoe Anthony Tukan, Sr.

But what America saw, most importantly, was a man, very cool, collective, and confident, a man, who did not lose his cool, even when his frustrated rival made an unnecessary attack on him.

Chapter Ten

INAUGURATION 2009

Dr. Huxtable is vindicated! His wife, Claire Huxtable, is also vindicated! And the show itself, the great Cosby Show, is very much avenged! May it now rest in peace, and forever be free from further criticism. Oh, well, whom am I really kidding? This is America. Is anybody, or any show ever free from criticism here?

Don't you remember when the Cosby Show first made its debut in 1984? From that year and for many consecutive years,it was the best comedy on television, at least according to me. Frankly, there was no competition. It truly always outscored its competitors, whatever they were. I was always so busy watching the Cosby Show every Thursday at 8:00 P.M., that I can not say what the competitors were at that very time.

The Cosby Show won so many awards in such a way that Bill Cosby, speaking on behalf of the cast, had refused further awards. He asked

147   **Jaytoe Anthony Tukan, Sr.**

TURNING OF THE TIDE

Hollywood to exclude their show from further nominations for awards. The Cosby Show was that good! It was a great family comedy.

Despite the success of the comedy, some critics did not really see the show as a true representation of real life. Some black people downplayed the show, indicating that, though this was an all-black cast, it did not represent the true black family in America. Others went so far in saying that the show was too 'white' to represent black people.

The Cosby Show was too 'white?' So how must a show really look, to represent a black family? Oh, I almost forgot! A black family, according to those critics, is never all that quiet. Black people fight; black people yell at each other, at their children, and even beat on their children. They do those terrible things that are very unheard of within any other race. In other words, white people are calmer, and much calmer. White people do not spank or beat on their children. Oh, no, white people do not ever yell at their children. Seriously, white people are perfect.

My friend, if you were to ask me to give you my interpretation of such comments about black people, I would say: black people do things that other human beings don't ever do. So, are black

Jaytoe Anthony Tukan, Sr.

TURNING OF THE TIDE

people human or what? Nope, black people are not human; they are not from planet earth.

Such an image, as portrayed by the Cosbys was too 'white' and unrealistic to be a black family. There were other critics who even said that black people are never that educated, like Dr. Huxtable, M.D., and his lawyer wife, Claire Huxtable, LL.D, to the point that both could be "white-collar" workers.

Woa! What absurdity can be worse than this! Talk about putting down a whole race of nations. With thinking like this, it is no wonder why many black children fail miserably in schools around the country. If the black elders are putting down the black race like this, is there any hope for black youngsters? Having this thought is one thing, but truly voicing it out like that? Does this bring the best out of black children? What inspiration does this offer to them?

Then comes the Obama family: two lawyers, two law professors, two 'white-collar' workers. Wait a minute! Wait a minute! By the way, the Obamas? They have children of their own, even though, not quite the number of children as on the Cosby Show. Hello? Anybody home?

Isn't the Obama family a good representation of the Cosby Show? Or should we not honestly ask a more realistic question? Isn't this Obama family,

Jaytoe Anthony Tukan, Sr.

TURNING OF THE TIDE

what the Cosby Show truly represented? Pray tell me, honestly. Do Michelle and Barack beat on their children? Is that what we hear from the crazy media?

Why do you ever think that black people are incapable to do what people from other races do? What lesson is that to black youngsters? Sadly to say, this is a negative message to hand down to our young people, for them, in turn, to hand down to their children. When does it ever stop? Why do we bring a curse on our own race, and still turn around to ask God why misfortune happens to black people?

~~~~~~~~~~

To the anticipation of nations around the world, the great day, Tuesday, January 20, 2009, had finally arrived. The whole world would definitely see the very first black President-Elect in America, Barack Obama, to be truly, truly inaugurated. But the previous day, Monday, January 19, 2009, was also another great day; it was the day the nation had just celebrated a National Holiday, the birth of Dr. Martin Luther King, Jr. I wonder what mood would Dr. King be in today? Wouldn't Martin be very ecstatic today to see a fulfillment of one of his predictions?

150 **Jaytoe Anthony Tukan, Sr.**

TURNING OF THE TIDE

"I have a dream that one day little black boys and black girls will be able to join hands with little white boys and white girls as sisters and brothers.....

"I have a dream that one day the sons of former slaves and the sons of former slave owners will be able to sit down together at the table of brotherhood ."

Isn't his wife, Coretta Scott-King reminding her husband right now, 'Martin, didn't I tell you to hang in there a little while longer? Look what's going on down there today!'

Dr. King believed the day would come when a black person would be a senator; he believed the day would come when a black person would also be a president of the United States of America.

"This will be the day when all of God's children will be able to sing with a new meaning, 'My country, 'tis of thee, sweet land of liberty, of thee I sing. Land where my fathers died, land of the pilgrims' pride, from every mountainside, let freedom ring.'"

That song was sung on that day by the Queen of Soul, Aretha Franklin, the very first black woman to be inducted into the Rock-n-Roll Hall of Fame. She stood before the nation and the whole world,

151 **Jaytoe Anthony Tukan, Sr.**

TURNING OF THE TIDE

and melodiously released those beautiful and ever important lines of the historic song, as the whole world was watching. This song had to be done just before the swearing-in ceremony. The man of the occasion, the President-Elect, had made the request to her Majesty, the Queen -- to sing the song before his inauguration.

What a day it was to see. Dr. King's dream, which is 'deeply rooted in the American dream,' had become a true reality. Finally, the President-Elect, Barack Hussein Obama, was sworn into office, becoming the 44th President of the great United States of America. Performing the historic ceremony was Honorable John Roberts, Chief Justice of the U.S. Supreme Court.

"I, Barack Obama, do solemnly swear (or affirm) that I will faithfully execute the office of President of the United States, and will to the best of my ability, preserve, protect and defend the Constitution of the United States. So help me, God."

After the swearing-in, President Barack Hussein Obama delivered his Inaugural Address to the nation, and to the world at large.

Jaytoe Anthony Tukan, Sr.

TURNING OF THE TIDE

"My fellow citizens:

"I stand here today humbled by the task before us, grateful for the trust you have bestowed, mindful of the sacrifices borne by our ancestors. I thank President Bush for his service to our nation --- (Applause), as well as the generosity and cooperation he has shown throughout this transition.

"Forty-four Americans have now taken the presidential oath. The words have been spoken during rising tides of prosperity and the still waters of peace. Yet, every so often, the oath is taken amidst gathering clouds and raging storms. At these moments, America has carried on not simply because of the skill or vision of those in high office, but because We the People have remained faithful to the ideals of our forebearers, and true to our founding documents.

"So it has been. So it must be with this generation of Americans. That we are in the midst of crisis is now well understood. Our nation is at war, against a far-reaching network of violence and hatred. Our economy is badly weakened, a consequence of greed and irresponsibility on the part of some, but also our collective failure to make hard choices and prepare the nation for a new age. Homes have been lost; jobs shed; businesses shuttered.

"Our health care is too costly; our schools fail too many; and each day brings further evidence that the ways we use energy strengthen our adversaries and threaten our planet. These are the indicators of crisis,

153   **Jaytoe Anthony Tukan, Sr.**

TURNING OF THE TIDE

subject to data and statistics. Less measurable but no less profound is a sapping of confidence across our land–a nagging fear that America's decline is inevitable, and that the next generation must lower its sights.

"Today I say to you that the challenges we face are real. They are serious and they are many. They will not be met easily or in a short span of time. But know this, America: They will be met. (Applause)

"On this day, we gather because we have chosen hope over fear, unity of purpose over conflict and discord. On this day, we come to proclaim an end to the petty grievances and false promises, the recriminations and worn-out dogmas, that for far too long have strangled our politics. We remain a young nation, but in the words of Scripture, the time has come to set aside childish things. The time has come to reaffirm our enduring spirit; to choose our better history; to carry forward that precious gift, that noble idea, passed on from generation to generation: the God-given promise that all are equal, all are free, and all deserve a chance to pursue their full measure of happiness. (Applause).

"In reaffirming the greatness of our nation, we understand that greatness is never a given. It must be earned. Our journey has never been one of shortcuts or settling for less. It has not been the path for the fainthearted -- for those who prefer leisure over work, or seek only the pleasures of riches and fame. Rather, it has been the risk-takers, the doers, the makers of things -- some celebrated, but more often men and women obscure

Jaytoe Anthony Tukan, Sr.

TURNING OF THE TIDE

in their labor -- who have carried us up the long, rugged path toward prosperity and freedom.

"For us, they packed up their few worldly possessions and traveled across oceans in search of a new life. For us, they toiled in sweatshops and settled the West; endured the lash of the whip and plowed the hard earth. For us, they fought and died, in places like Concord and Gettysburg; Normandy and Khe Sahn.

"Time and again, these men and women struggled and sacrificed and worked till their hands were raw so that we might live a better life. They saw America as bigger than the sum of our individual ambitions; greater than all the differences of birth or wealth or faction.

"This is the journey we continue today. We remain the most prosperous, powerful nation on Earth. Our workers are no less productive than when this crisis began. Our minds are no less inventive, our goods and services no less needed than they were last week or last month or last year. Our capacity remains undiminished. But our time of standing pat, of protecting narrow interests and putting off unpleasant decisions -- that time has surely passed. Starting today, we must pick ourselves up, dust ourselves off, and begin again the work of remaking America. (Applause).

"For everywhere we look, there is work to be done. The state of the economy calls for action, bold and swift, and we will act -- not only to create new jobs, but to lay a new foundation for growth. We will build the roads and bridges, the electric grids and digital lines

155   **Jaytoe Anthony Tukan, Sr.**

TURNING OF THE TIDE

that feed our commerce and bind us together. We will restore science to its rightful place, and wield technology's wonders to raise health care's quality and lower its cost. We will harness the sun and the winds and the soil to fuel our cars and run our factories. And we will transform our schools and colleges and universities to meet the demands of a new age. All this we can do. And all this we will do.

"Now, there are some who question the scale of our ambitions -- who suggest that our system cannot tolerate too many big plans. Their memories are short. For they have forgotten what this country has already done; what free men and women can achieve when imagination is joined to common purpose, and necessity to courage. What the cynics fail to understand is that the ground has shifted beneath them -- that the stale political arguments that have consumed us for so long no longer apply.

"The question we ask today is not whether our government is too big or too small, but whether it works -- whether it helps families find jobs at a decent wage, care they can afford, a retirement that is dignified. Where the answer is yes, we intend to move forward. Where the answer is no, programs will end. And those of us who manage the public's dollars will be held to account -- to spend wisely, reform bad habits, and do our business in the light of day -- because only then can we restore the vital trust between a people and their government.

Jaytoe Anthony Tukan, Sr.

TURNING OF THE TIDE

"Nor is the question before us whether the market is a force for good or ill. Its power to generate wealth and expand freedom is unmatched, but this crisis has reminded us that without a watchful eye, the market can spin out of control -- and that a nation cannot prosper long when it favors only the prosperous. The success of our economy has always depended not just on the size of our gross domestic product, but on the reach of our prosperity; on our ability to extend opportunity to every willing heart -- not out of charity, but because it is the surest route to our common good. (Applause).

"As for our common defense, we reject as false the choice between our safety and our ideals. Our Founding Fathers, faced with perils we can scarcely imagine, drafted a charter to assure the rule of law and the rights of man, a charter expanded by the blood of generations. Those ideals still light the world, and we will not give them up for expedience's sake. (Applause).

"And so to all other peoples and governments who are watching today, from the grandest capitals to the small village where my father was born: Know that America is a friend of each nation and every man, woman and child who seeks a future of peace and dignity, and that we are ready to lead once more. (Applause).

"Recall that earlier generations faced down fascism and communism not just with missiles and tanks, but with sturdy alliances and enduring convictions. They

Jaytoe Anthony Tukan, Sr.

TURNING OF THE TIDE

understood that our power alone cannot protect us, nor does it entitle us to do as we please. Instead, they knew that our power grows through its prudent use; our security emanates from the justness of our cause, the force of our example, the tempering qualities of humility and restraint.

"We are the keepers of this legacy. Guided by these principles once more, we can meet those new threats that demand even greater effort-- even greater cooperation and understanding between nations. We will begin to responsibly leave Iraq to its people, and forge a hard-earned peace in Afghanistan. With old friends and former foes, we will work tirelessly to lessen the nuclear threat, and roll back the specter of a warming planet.

"We will not apologize for our way of life, nor will we waver in its defense, and for those who seek to advance their aims by inducing terror and slaughtering innocents, we say to you now that our spirit is stronger and cannot be broken; you cannot outlast us, and we will defeat you. (Applause).

"For we know that our patchwork heritage is a strength, not a weakness. We are a nation of Christians and Muslims, Jews and Hindus -- and nonbelievers. We are shaped by every language and culture, drawn from every end of this Earth; and because we have tasted the bitter swill of civil war and segregation, and emerged from that dark chapter stronger and more united, we cannot help but believe that the old hatreds shall

Jaytoe Anthony Tukan, Sr.

TURNING OF THE TIDE

someday pass; that the lines of tribe shall soon dissolve; that as the world grows smaller, our common humanity shall reveal itself; and that America must play its role in ushering in a new era of peace.

"To the Muslim world, we seek a new way forward, based on mutual interest and mutual respect. To those leaders around the globe who seek to sow conflict, or blame their society's ills on the West: Know that your people will judge you on what you can build, not what you destroy. (Applause).

"To those who cling to power through corruption and deceit and the silencing of dissent, know that you are on the wrong side of history; but that we will extend a hand if you are willing to unclench your fist. (Applause).

"To the people of poor nations, we pledge to work alongside you to make your farms flourish and let clean waters flow; to nourish starved bodies and feed hungry minds. And to those nations like ours that enjoy relative plenty, we say we can no longer afford indifference to suffering outside our borders; nor can we consume the world's resources without regard to effect. For the world has changed, and we must change with it.

"As we consider the road that unfolds before us, we remember with humble gratitude those brave Americans who, at this very hour, patrol far-off deserts and distant mountains. They have something to tell us today, just as the fallen heroes who lie in Arlington whisper through the ages. We honor them not only

159   **Jaytoe Anthony Tukan, Sr.**

TURNING OF THE TIDE

because they are guardians of our liberty, but because they embody the spirit of service; a willingness to find meaning in something greater than themselves. And yet, at this moment -- a moment that will define a generation -- it is precisely this spirit that must inhabit us all.

"For as much as government can do and must do, it is ultimately the faith and determination of the American people upon which this nation relies. It is the kindness to take in a stranger when the levees break, the selflessness of workers who would rather cut their hours than see a friend lose their job which sees us through our darkest hours. It is the firefighter's courage to storm a stairway filled with smoke, but also a parent's willingness to nurture a child, that finally decides our fate.

"Our challenges may be new. The instruments with which we meet them may be new. But those values upon which our success depends -- hard work and honesty, courage and fair play, tolerance and curiosity, loyalty and patriotism -- these things are old. These things are true. They have been the quiet force of progress throughout our history. What is demanded then is a return to these truths.

"What is required of us now is a new era of responsibility -- a recognition, on the part of every American, that we have duties to ourselves, our nation and the world; duties that we do not grudgingly accept but rather seize gladly, firm in the knowledge that there

Jaytoe Anthony Tukan, Sr.

TURNING OF THE TIDE

is nothing so satisfying to the spirit, so defining of our character, than giving our all to a difficult task. This is the price and the promise of citizenship. This is the source of our confidence -- the knowledge that God calls on us to shape an uncertain destiny. This is the meaning of our liberty and our creed--why men and women and children of every race and every faith can join in celebration across this magnificent Mall, and why a man whose father less than 60 years ago might not have been served at a local restaurant can now stand before you to take a most sacred oath. (Applause).

"So let us mark this day with remembrance, of who we are and how far we have traveled. In the year of America's birth, in the coldest of months, a small band of patriots huddled by dying campfires on the shores of an icy river. The capital was abandoned. The enemy was advancing. The snow was stained with blood. At a moment when the outcome of our revolution was most in doubt, the father of our nation ordered these words be read to the people:

"'Let it be told to the future world ... that in the depth of winter, when nothing but hope and virtue could survive... that the city and the country, alarmed at one common danger, came forth to meet it.'"

"America. In the face of our common dangers, in this winter of our hardship, let us remember these timeless words. With hope and virtue, let us brave once more the icy currents, and endure what storms may

Jaytoe Anthony Tukan, Sr.

come. Let it be said by our children's children that when we were tested, we refused to let this journey end, that we did not turn back, nor did we falter; and with eyes fixed on the horizon and God's grace upon us, we carried forth that great gift of freedom and delivered it safely to future generations.

"Thank you. God bless you. And God bless the United States of America." (Applause).

Chapter Eleven

Universal Health Insurance

O ther world citizens envy America for its free-for-all society. They truly think because the United States of America is a democratic country, any decision made by the president is easily acceptable to all the citizens, but the reality could not be farther from the truth. Very unpopular decisions or proposals from the White House are very often subject to challenges and/or debates by the United States Congress, and also by some of the citizens throughout the country, at which time so much friction, and too many harsh words can develop on all sides. This display of exercising one's rights leads us to the fact that Democracy is still going to be the government of the people, for the

Jaytoe Anthony Tukan, Sr.

TURNING OF THE TIDE

people, and by the people. A true democracy, therefore, must always allow the people (the governed), to freely elect their leader (the governor). Because of this freedom of exercising their rights within such a democratic society, citizens can definitely disagree or oppose any legislation, and make their disagreements known through arguments or debates, without any fear of reprisal from their leader.

Adding to the meaning of democracy, or simply to make sure that democracy works well, wherever it seems to exist, a great Liberian historian, Mr. Ernest Jerome Yancy, writes, "Democracy is necessary because man is a brute, and if given his own way, he will use his brutality against his fellow men." For this very reason, citizens need a democratic government. So it is not that simple to arrive at any decision, or even more so, create any legislation, absolutely free of challenges in the United States, contrary to the thinking of other world citizens about America.

During the Clinton Presidency, he and his wife, Hillary, tried to bring about the same universal health insurance, but it did not work. Mrs. Clinton received so much criticism for that matter. As if President Obama is unaware of the Clinton

Jaytoe Anthony Tukan, Sr.

TURNING OF THE TIDE

administration's failure to bring universal health care to America, he, too, has decided to embark upon this same difficult journey.

While most of those we interviewed see the President's insurance program as a good plan for America, some still think it is a waste of tax payers' dollars. Now the new U.S. Congress is trying to repeal the bill, though the plan is already helping some citizens. Will repealing the bill work? Are the citizens, especially those who currently benefit from the plan, going to stand by idly while Congress kills the bill?

Others have even suggested that because President Obama is black, he will always have an uphill battle with Congress in whatever goals he tries to achieve. Christie, one of the interviewees even remarked, "Being the race that he is, he is going to have to work very, very hard to accomplish anything........"

To this comment, Dean, another interviewee, replied that the president "is going to do what he was set to do, regardless."

Ask Anna, who also directed her own question back at us: "Do you want to live in a country where you will be walking in the street and see a sick person who tells you that because he does

165   **Jaytoe Anthony Tukan, Sr.**

not have medical insurance or money, he can not get a doctor? Is that the kind of country you want to live in?"

These interviews were conducted on the street corners and the marketplace. Some were relatively sometimes also conducted at the interviewees' job sites.

Tammie, a black lady, possibly mid 40s, said this about the President's Plan. "I think it's an outstanding plan, especially for single parents. Sometimes when your children are not in college, but having trouble finding a job, they need to be insured. I just hate that it doesn't include grandchildren, and other people that live with you as well."

David, white, about 40 years old, had colon cancer, and is now undergoing an after-surgery therapy. He doesn't seem too cool about universal health care, which he refers to as 'the government plan.' First, he doesn't think that the government can run anything well. Secondly, David doubts if he will ever get any treatment under this plan, comparable to what he receives from his current insurance company.

"It's a good thing....The bad part about it is,

TURNING OF THE TIDE

as years go by, if the cancer comes back, will I be treated or not?."

"But that's what he says, the president, that pre-existing condition will not be a reason to deny you," I said to David.

"Right, it won't be a reason to deny me, but it doesn't mean that I'm going to get treated," said David. Continuing, "That's not a guarantee.... After a couple of years from now, if everything goes to... the government plan, I don't think 1 will get that treatment. I think I will get that treatment after I die."

Very shocked to hear David make such a statement, I asked him, "You're gonna what?"

"I will get that treatment after I die," David emphatically repeated himself.

I asked, "What? I mean why? I mean, insurance," as I found myself baffling for words here.

"They're already starting that now; they're already starting to back off on some of the drugs and everything, and it is going to cost so much. They're going to start making efficiency moves. Efficiency moves means in a lot of cases, take away treatments..... But they're going to start taking it from the doctors' hands, and start putting it into the

Jaytoe Anthony Tukan, Sr.

TURNING OF THE TIDE

politicians' hands," David indicated.

"Is that what you're thinking?" Again, still surprised, I asked David.

Here again, he said, "Yes, and I think that the government can't run anything well."

Josephine, black, a school teacher, probably in her mid 30s, looks at the insurance issue from two different angles. She said, "I do not really mind health insurance for all Americans. My major concern is that there are some people who do not want to work, like my brother, for example. He's 40 years old, still lives at home with our mom, but physically, there is nothing wrong with him. Why should tax payers pay his medical bills?"

"You've got a point there, too. But you are not totally against the idea of universal health insurance, are you?" I asked the teacher.

"No, not at all. I think it is good....., to keep America healthy. But there are some people who just want to receive; they do not ever want to give anything back. Having said that, I think it will still be good to have, because I have a friend right now who is retired. Her medical bills are more than her retirement money. So it would be good to have

Jaytoe Anthony Tukan, Sr.

TURNING OF THE TIDE

universal health insurance," Josephine further indicated.

Brian, white, 28-years old, who lost his manufacturing job, currently has two part-time jobs, but does not have health insurance. He says, "I think in the long run, it's a good thing that everybody have health insurance, affordable health insurance. I don't have health insurance right now. It will be good to have it. I'm still young, too."

"You're about 25 (or so)?" I asked Brian.

"Yea, I am 28," Brian, who appeared to have a positive outlook about life, indicated.

"You just graduated from college?" I asked again.

"Yea; I was in manufacturing, but I lost my job from there."

"Everybody in America needs health insurance," says Pam, a black lady, maybe in her late 40s, a school bus driver. Pam does not have any dependents, as her children are grown and on their own. So she practically gets free health insurance. On the other hand, she feels for her co-worker, another bus driver, who pays $300 every month for her and her four children. She does not earn much.

Jaytoe Anthony Tukan, Sr.

TURNING OF THE TIDE

"But then everybody can not afford health insurance," I said to Pam.

"Exactly!" She agreed.

"And that's what the president is dong, by trying to create health insurance for everybody, affordable health insurance. So why is it that people are fighting him? Why don't they want that?" I asked Pam again.

Pam said, "I don't know, I don't think that, but...some people are gonna complain about everything you do, regardless. See what I'm saying?"

"I see what you're saying, Pam." Furthermore, I introduced some part of the conversation I had with Josephine, who said that there are some people who can work, but do not want to work. She used her brother as an example. Why should tax payers pay for his insurance?

"Now that's true," Pam agreed. Then she continued, "There are people out there that don't work, can't work. But I can see them getting insurance, the ones that want to work, but just can't find the job, or are not able to work. But these lazy people that're sitting around waiting for a check, and waiting on somebody to give them health care, that's not fair....."

Jaytoe Anthony Tukan, Sr.

TURNING OF THE TIDE

Tony, black, about 30 years old, agrees that everyone deserves healthcare, but he sees the opposition differently. "I think because it's taking money away from them. But au...I think everybody deserves a little something, especially when it comes to health care."

Albert, black, possibly 35 years old, sees the opposition to the health insurance from a racial point of view. "To be honest with you, I think it's the whole racial thing. They don't want to see a black person trying to do something good for a change, discrimination against everybody. But at the end of the day, it's going to help the same people, black, white, Hispanic, everybody here."

Tom, white, a retiree from the airline, weighed in. "With my retirement money, I can hardly afford my medical bills. So, I think it would be good if all of us were insured under this program."

I inquired of Tom, "You are retired right now, so it seems difficult to pay your full medical expenses. But if you were still working like you used to do, how would you feel about universal health care?"

Jaytoe Anthony Tukan, Sr.

TURNING OF THE TIDE

"I would still want everyone to have medical insurance. But let me ask you a question of my own. The car you drive today, don't you know that you are paying for uninsured motorists?" Tom asked me.

"That much I know. What's the point that you are trying to make?" I answered Tom's question, with a follow-up question of mine to him.

"If the insured drivers are paying for the uninsured drivers, wouldn't it be much better if all drivers were really insured and paying for themselves?"

"Definitely, that would be great. That way, I wouldn't have to pay for anyone," I answered Tom.

"That's exactly the point that Mr. Obama is making. If all Americans were insured under his affordable insurance plan, with the government helping out with a minimum amount for each person who could not pay for himself, then you and I would not have to pay so much for other people as we do now for uninsured motorists."

Somehow Tom makes a lot of sense, but I switched gear to a different direction totally, going a little personal with him. "Did you vote for Mr. Obama? Is he your favorite guy."

"Favorite or not, it doesn't matter. To be

172   **Jaytoe Anthony Tukan, Sr.**

TURNING OF THE TIDE

honest with you, I did not vote for Mr. Obama. I voted for Mr. John McCain. But this health plan that President Obama is proposing makes sense to me. I don't see why everybody is not embracing that."

Anna, white, about late 40s, is also in favor of the President's universal health insurance. "I think everybody needs health care. I think it's very important."

"So if everybody needs health care, and all these people know about it, why is he getting so much opposition about that?" I asked Anna.

"I think because it's got to be financed from somewhere, you know; times are tight. But you're going to have to pay for it one way or another. It's not going to change. And the folks that have more aught to be able to help those who don't."

Somehow I tried to introduce to Anna, some of Tom's statements, indicating that drivers who have auto insurance do actually pay for drivers who don't have insurance. So why won't Americans do the same thing for one another when it comes to health care? In other words, "Nothing is free."

Anna agrees "That's correct......that hasn't changed. What you're going to do? Deny people the right to have any care? There's something wrong

Jaytoe Anthony Tukan, Sr.

there. Is that the kind of country you want to live in? Do you want to live in a country where people (doctors) will turn people away because they couldn't afford a doctor....?"

"And by doing this, other people are accusing him, Sarah Palin, for example, that he's moving us towards socialism. Do you believe that? Socialism, where everybody has everything, but nobody owns anything,"

I asked Anna, who so patiently took the time to answer every question methodically.

"No, I don't think so, because this has always been a capitalist society. You might have some things that appear to be that way, like Medicaid and Medicare. But then it was a democratic republic. To people who don't understand what a democratic republic is...., we are founded to be a democratic republic. Granted, times have changed, but I don't think we will go away from having a capitalist society. Calling it socialist is inappropriate, because socialism is more than just medicine. That's also politics; that's also economics. And we aren't that way, and I don't think we will ever be economically that way......."

Next I asked Ty, a black young lady, maybe

TURNING OF THE TIDE

25 years old, "Do you think it's a good thing that all Americans have health insurance?"   `

"Yea, I think it will be a good thing, Ty answered."

"If it is a good thing, why is he getting so much opposition?" I asked.

"I just don't think they want him to succeed at what he's trying to do."

"Is it because he's black?" I put the young lady on the spot here.

"Honestly, I think it is; I just feel that way," she replied.

Somehow I tried to bring in some part of the conversation I had with Anna, who wonders if she wants to live in a country where doctors turn patients away because they do not have health insurance or money. Anna wonders if that's the kind of country we want to have?

"No, but right now I feel like that's the kind of country we have," Ty said. "Off course they (doctors) want to say they'll help you. But on actuality, it's way more than they can do. But because you don't have health insurance...., they only do the minimum. And I feel like...it's a life. There should not be a price on a life."

Ty further emphasized that because Obama is

TURNING OF THE TIDE

a black president, they want to give him a hard way to go. "I think that they are giving him a whole lot of problems because of the fact that he is a black president, and he's not a quitter.... He's going to continue to fight, whether they want to hear him or not, he's going to be heard, and I'm behind him one hundred percent. Whatever my president wants, I want!"

Next I asked Tanya, a black lady, who may be in her mid 40s; she sees the health insurance issue differently. "It depends, you know; it will work for some people, but it won't work for all. Everyone's situation is different. But no one should have to have insurance."

Surprised, I wondered if no one should have to have insurance, "How are people going to pay for their health?"

"I mean there's (a) bunch of people that's paying for insurance right now. I'm paying for insurance for my health and my family health. But my claim gets denied. It has to be a specific reason why they wouldn't accept my claim...When it comes to that aspect of it, I believe that no one should have to have insurance."

I agreed with Tanya, that if her claim gets

Jaytoe Anthony Tukan, Sr.

TURNING OF THE TIDE

denied every time, then there is really no need to be paying for insurance.

She went on, "Just like car insurance, house insurance, I mean we had the flood with the hails, and a lot of people, including myself, were denied.... I've had insurance for my home for eleven years. I've well paid more than my share."

"They denied you?" I asked Tanya. What could be the reason for denying her?

"Yea, they denied me. They said I did not have enough damage... Here it is, I'm paying all this money for insurance to help me.... But when I need the help, that's when the door is slammed. It's not fair for those who're paying (for) insurance. "

Here was a lady who had homeowner insurance with Allstate, but her claim was turned down, because her house was not damaged to the point that they (Allstate) should have to fix it. Come on, now, the roof was damaged. Tanya and her family had to pay $7,000 out of pocket to fix the roof. There is always an excuse from insurance companies when it comes to meeting their end of the bargain.

Johnnie, a black lady, probably about 45 years old, had this to say: "Yea, I think everybody should

Jaytoe Anthony Tukan, Sr.

TURNING OF THE TIDE

have health insurance, because they go to the hospital, (and) they get turned around. And some of them don't feel they've been treated fair."

I stressed to Johnnie that the President continues to get opposition not just from Congress, but from some citizens across the country. "Why?"

She replied, "Because we're still living in the country who have not been able to see fairness in every nationality..... Some people are wealthy; some people're not; some people, who're - in between, they feel that they want to hold unto their money rather than helping somebody else..... So that's the problem we have in this country. We claim that we are moving forward, but then yet, we're still trying to hold each other back."

Then there was Jessica, white, a high school teacher, maybe 35 years old, who also looks at the health plan differently. "It sounds like socialism to me: everybody gets everything free from the government, but nobody really owns anything. Is that the kind of United States we want to live in now?"

"So you truly believe we are leading towards a socialist society here? You think this capitalist society will ever change?" I asked Jessica.

Jaytoe Anthony Tukan, Sr.

TURNING OF THE TIDE

"I mean I really do not think the U.S. will be that way, but it sounds, to me, like socialism. Don't get me wrong; I voted for President Obama. But on this one, I don't know. I really don't know."

Laura and William, a white couple, possibly in their early 40s, also favor the President's Universal Health Plan. "I think it was necessary; I think everybody should have insurance." said Laura. She also added that "the government should have a scale, based on your income." She does not think anyone should be penalized just because they could not participate in the insurance plan.

I also asked Laura the same question that I posed to everyone else, everyone who thought this plan was good for America. "Why are people opposing it?"

She replied, "I think it's the idea and the concept that they have to conform to being told that they must do this. I think that humanly, we rise against someone telling us we have no choice. It sounds like dictatorship, which it's not meant to be that. But I mean, we have to have car insurance. Nobody's rising up against that."

I added, "And then we're paying for uninsured motorists."

Jaytoe Anthony Tukan, Sr.

TURNING OF THE TIDE

"Right, right. I think we need health insurance; we all need to be insured. There are people that have lesser income that can not afford the insurance; that I think it would help the social system..if everybody have insurance, then you don't have so many people on medicaid."

"Right, then medicaid would not be struggling; those who really need it would have it," I agreed with Laura.

"Who's paying for the bunch of the taxes? It's the working class people. I mean, the higher level income..if you have, there's all kinds of tax breaks, and tax cuts, and tax shelters..." Laura said. She went on, "You have money, you make money, you keep money. But the middle class, you normally don't have health insurance, and you're struggling to pay for insurance. I mean, we pay over $3,000 a year to have health insurance for two people."

"Wow!" I exclaimed.

William also weighed in, "Then you still have all your deductibles............."

William mentioned further that he needed to do an MRI for his arthritis in the neck. But the insurance company does not cover MRI. The procedure costs $800. "So I've got to pay $800. Now $800 for someone in the upper income bracket,

Jaytoe Anthony Tukan, Sr.

TURNING OF THE TIDE

no problem. But to us, that's a lot of money. So, I say well, I can't do that now. What do you do?"

Laura comes back, "I have a roommate right now, who has muscular dystrophy... Her shots are over $1,100 a month. Her income is only $1,200 a month. Nobody, nobody will insure her. Nobody will insure her," she emphasized.

"And that's bad," I answered, as I began to feel sorry for Laura's roommate.

"That's bad," Laura added.

William, putting aside his own health issues, is very passionate about America's elderly people, for whom he says that the government has never done much. "We are the richest country in the world; our elderly are out here on the street without health care, or paying every dime that they got from retirement. We ought to hang our head in shame....................."

Laura further indicated, "And they can't afford medicine. The one thing the health care plan will do, it will prevent people (from denying any coverage to others) like my roommate, she will be able to have insurance; she will be able to get treatment. The elderly, like he was saying, will be able to afford their medication. I'm all for it. I think Obama did good. I mean, he took a stand (against) a

181 **Jaytoe Anthony Tukan, Sr.**

TURNING OF THE TIDE

lot of people. A lot of people didn't like that. But for the middle class working people, we're all going Yeh! Yeh! Yeh!"

William added, "Here is the other problem I have. The whole system is broken....the whole system is broken.... Obama isn't going to wipe out special interest groups; he isn't going to wipe out lobbyists, who spend millions of dollars; he's not going to wipe out pharmaceutical companies who fail to develop a cheaper drugs on the market, to help treat cancer and other diseases....."

Darren & Christie, an interracial couple probably in their late 20s, with their two beautiful daughters, also weighed. "I think it is a good think, said Christie."

Darren agreed, "Absolutely, it is a good thing, but I will believe it when I see it. I like Obama, but he n't impress me yet."

About other people opposing the plan, Darren said, "Nobody wants him to get any further. They don't care whether he does a good job or not. Nobody wants him to succeed. He's got to overwork himself to accomplish anything."

Christie added, "Not only that. I think Bush has done so much....now it takes a lot to undo

Jaytoe Anthony Tukan, Sr.

everything. It's screwed up!"

"Right, and they are blaming him already for the bad economy," I indicated to the couple.

Christie followed up, "Also being the race (black race) that he is, a lot of people are expecting him to fail, or want him to fail. He is going to have to work very, very hard to accomplish anything."

Linda and Deborah, both black, maybe daughter and mom, shared their views as well. "People need health insurance," said Linda.

"So everybody should get insurance?" I asked Linda, who said, "Yes, everybody should have health insurance."

About the opposition to the President's Health Plan, Deborah, 63, said, "Because of a change in time; people don't like to change. People being a certain way, you always have to fight to change. It is the change; everybody needs health insurance. So we do have to change, because to me, if you don't change, you gonna be left behind......."

Dean, a black lady, probably 30 years old, also favors the President's insurance plan. "Because they feel that if you don't have it now, you couldn't afford it, and it will be coming out of my pocket for you to have.   That's why they are opposing it. Because they have it, and they have it for their children, and they have it for their children's children......"

"In any society, there are the haves and the have-nots. So now the haves don't want to share with the have-nots?" I observed.

She replied, "Off course not! They don't think we're worthy of it. they don't think we're worthy of it."

Dean further believes that anything that the president does, "If it is of no advantage to them, they're going to oppose it. They'll keep opposing it...."

Big John, black, about 25 years old, says he also likes the President's plan. When asked why he thinks some people are opposed to this plan, he says "Because nobody else, nobody else ever got it passed. He's the only one that ever got it passed. Since he got it passed, the tug is on his back since he got it passed......"

"They don't want to give him the credit," I interjected.

"They don't want to give him the credit. They don't want to give him the credit, because what he

TURNING OF THE TIDE

now did, he now did something that (had) never been done." Big John added.

"Not even all the white presidents, Clinton tried it; it did not work. Instead of helping him to see it through, they're going to all oppose to it," I added.

"Yea," Big John agreed. Then added, "Nobody ain't ever come close to having it. So when he did...., just like common knowledge. But it's a good thing, and I am all for it; I'm glad it happened."

These are some of the stories I listened to, as I went from one street corner to the other, from one marketplace to another. These are U.S. citizens speaking from their hearts about a single issue affecting everybody. They are not foreigners; they are Americans, who can not afford health insurance. Ninety-nine per cent of those interviewed, are all in favor of the health plan, the President's Universal Health Insurance.

So I ask you, my dear reader, is there something wrong with all Americans being medically insured? What could be the harm in creating a healthy America? As Americans, we can get up from our beds, jump on the airplane to some

Jaytoe Anthony Tukan, Sr.

TURNING OF THE TIDE

foreign land to help its citizens in a great disaster. But what's wrong with us helping our own? What's wrong with us, Americans, helping one another by paying an extra $5 or $10 a month for another American to get a chance to a doctor?

We help others away from our soil, yet we would not help our own? One of the interviewees, Anna, has already answered that question, by asking every American:

"What you're going to do? Deny people the right to have any care? There's something wrong there. Is that the kind of country you want to live in?"

Jaytoe Anthony Tukan, Sr.

Chapter Twelve

Is Terrorism Dead?

"Good evening. Tonight, I can report to the American people and to the world that the United States has conducted an operation that killed Osama bin Laden, the leader of Al Qaida, and a terrorist who's responsible for the murder of thousands of innocent men, women, and children."

Those were the words of the President of the United States of America, Barack Obama. The President delivered the news from the White House, shortly before midnight on May 1, 2011.America had waited for a long time for this news. Now it happened. Relieved, the President, in no uncertain terms, told the nation and the world that Osama bin Laden, the world's Number One terrorist, came tumbling down. What a relief it was for thousands and thousands of Americans in the country, and around the world.

Jaytoe Anthony Tukan, Sr.

TURNING OF THE TIDE

A president of action, not words. I believe many of us still recall that on January 20, 2009, a few minutes after taking the Oath of Office, President Obama immediately sent a message to the terrorist world, and promised America that terrorism would not be tolerated, and it will be defeated. He said in his Inaugural Address, "We will not apologize for our way of life, nor will we waver in its defense. And for those who seek to advance their aims by inducing terror and slaughtering innocents, we say to you now that our spirit is stronger and cannot be broken; you cannot outlast us, and we will defeat you."

On the night of May 1, 2011, the American people saw that a portion of that promise was kept. On this night, the Commander-in-Chief of the U.S. Military had this to say, "Today, at my direction, the United States launched a targeted operation against that compound (Osama's safe haven), in Abbottabad, Pakistan. A small team of Americans carried out the operation with extraordinary courage and capability. No Americans were harmed. They took care to avoid civilian casualties. After a firefight, they killed Osama bin Laden and took custody of his body."

Jaytoe Anthony Tukan, Sr.

TURNING OF THE TIDE

If you have been reading this book chapter-by-chapter, you may still remember that in chapter one, I described the president as a farsighted, results-driven leader. And in another section of the book, I referred to him as cool, collective, and will not urge our military men and women to war, unless America's back was pushed against the wall. Well, collectively, our nation's back has been pushed against the wall for more than ten years since that fateful day of September 11, 2001.

The decision of the administration to take on bin Laden should send a clear message to the entire Al Qaeda organization that terrorism, in any shape or form, and whether within our borders or across the globe, will not be tolerated. Such a decision shows courage and a firm commitment by the president to our common cause and existence as a nation.

I am not a soldier, nor do I understand wars, but I have seen many casualties and destructions caused by wars. I can still see, and it is my belief that many Americans do also see today, the flashing images of September 11, 2001, before our eyes, when about three thousand of our citizens lost their lives. And who had been bragging about this? Was it not bin Laden? Is it not his Al Qaeda organization which

Jaytoe Anthony Tukan, Sr.

still plans to attack America?

So now that Osama is dead, does this end the danger and threat of terrorism? Is terrorism dead? The president answers those questions by warning us as a nation, to keep our protective armor on, not to let it off for a second. The war on terror is not over.

"For over two decades, bin Laden has been Al Qaeda's leader and symbol, and has continued to plot attacks against our country and our friends and allies. The death of bin Laden marks the most significant achievement to date in our nation's effort to defeat Al Qaeda.

"Yet his death does not mark the end of our effort. There's no doubt that Al Qaeda will continue to pursue attacks against us. We must and we will remain vigilant at home and abroad."

So the Pakistanis did not know? Yea, right, tell me another story; I won't believe this one. It is very much astonishing that Pakistan, an ally of the United States, does claim that it had no knowledge about bin Laden living well in that country for about five to six years. His hideout compound right next door to the Pakistani military base? How could that be?

TURNING OF THE TIDE

Like many of us, CIA Director, Leon Panetta also wondered about this. He commented that 'Pakistan had to know about Osama bin Laden living in the country, or the Pakistanis were incompetent to do the job.'

So what could it be, Pakistanis? Must America trust you again? 'Incompetence or no knowledge,' the bottom line is this: the job was not done.

So I ask, you, America, should we continue to trust Pakistan? Is the relationship between our two countries now in jeopardy?

The President's action to bring down bin Laden very well exemplifies leadership. A great leadership is not just talking the talk, but walking the walk. In other words, it must be a leadership of action, and not just words.

President Barack is still 'Committed To Service, Despite Adversities.'

Jaytoe Anthony Tukan, Sr.

EPILOGUE

The African family tree is very large. So it is not surprising for a person like me, who grew up within the African culture, to encounter a large family like the Obamas.

In life, we build bridges; we tear down unsaved bridges; we follow the footsteps of others, while creating our own footprints that we leave behind. We try to make straight the crooked places we see; we try to make a difference by helping another person in need. These all sum up to one word: Life. Life that we live and how we live it - must speak volumes for us, while still here on earth, or after we make our final exit from this world. What remains of us must be a legacy that others may remember about us, and perhaps emulate.

The Obama Family Tree has been in existence, long before the Europeans set foot on Kenyan soil. As such, a single writer like me can not even begin to embark upon the journey of writing a family story to its completeness, unless I intended to being an overnight historian, or a genius of some sort. That I honestly do not claim to be. What I have tried to do, however, is piece apart a portion of that

Jaytoe Anthony Tukan, Sr.

TURNING OF THE TIDE

great family tree, and show to somebody what I have found. It is my hope I have done that.

The Obama Family story is a true human story of two cultures, with two continental connections, well blended to form a unified bound. From these two distinctive cultures, evolved a great generation of subcultures, which developed into yet a community of families, some of whom, though they had not yet seen one another, still held a unified family tie.

This book will end, yet by going back to the beginning, and to the very first day, the Patriarch, Hussein Onyango, silently and lovingly, pronounced blessings upon his young son, about to be air-lifted into a new world. It was a new and different world, whose culture and peoples, young Barack, a 23-year-old student, really knew nothing about in 1959. But he would soon learn.

Their connecting dots, that of the Obamas, and that of the Dunhams, began in a Russian Language class on a college campus. Neither he (Barack), nor she (Ann), could have envisioned at the time that their affection for each other would ever amount to anything more. Nevertheless, those tiny feelings for each other grew stronger and stronger, and somehow generated into something

Jaytoe Anthony Tukan, Sr.

TURNING OF THE TIDE

bigger, or something much dipper than the couple's own imagination.

From that very continental union, we see a great generation of two family trees and two peoples, so separated by the Atlantic Ocean, so far way from each other, yet close enough that distance, race, ethnicity, nationality, religion, or political ideologies, could not keep them apart.

The wisdom of the elders is indispensable. Therefore, when youngsters are given sound counsel by an elder, youngsters must take heed. When the great Patriarch, Onyango (in Africa), received a letter from his son, Hussein Obama (in America), asking for the father's blessings to marry Ann, a white American girl he had met, the elder had an objection. Ann's father was not too cool with the idea, either. Foreseeing that the future for the young couple did not look too promising, Hussein Onyango raised his concern in no uncertain terms.

Telling his son about responsibilities at home, Mr. Onyango warned, in a letter, that it was not a good idea for his son to marry to a white woman. "How can you marry this white woman when (you know that) you already have responsibilities at home? Will this woman return with you and live as

Jaytoe Anthony Tukan, Sr.

TURNING OF THE TIDE

a Luo woman? Will she accept that you already have a wife and children? I have not heard of white people understanding such things. Their women are jealous and used to being pampered..."[6]

In other words, the culture from Kansas, blended with the Kenyan Luo culture - would someday clash, and the result would be a strong chilling effect on all parties involved, including the couple's offsprings. Despite the warning from Obama's father, together with the fact that Ann's parents also had reservation, the couple went ahead and got married.

After Hussein Obama returned to Kenya at the completion of his study in the United States, there followed after him, a white woman. One would think that this woman was Ann, Barack's mother. But she was not Ann; rather, she was Ruth. Obama, Sr. told his father (Onyango) that he was surprised to see Ruth follow him, as she was just a lady he had met while doing his graduate study at Harvard; he further indicated that there was no such an agreement between him and Ruth. His father never believed the story; he felt that his son's ill-responsible behavior

---

[6]

Dreams from My Father, (Barack Obama, 2005).

Jaytoe Anthony Tukan, Sr.

TURNING OF THE TIDE

had once again been proven. Despite his denial of a consent between him and Ruth, Obama ended up marrying Ruth. But after their wedding, Ruth would want nothing to do with Obama's children: Auma and Roy, by his African wife, Kezia. Ruth refused to have the children live with the couple.

The wisdom of the Patriarch, Onyango, together with his advice and warning to his son, had now come to pass. It goes without saying, youngsters must pay heed to the sound counsel of the elders.

Some may wonder: had Obama taken Ann and their baby to Kenya, would Ann behave as Ruth did, not allowing his children by his African wife, to live with the couple?

To answer that question, one needs to stop and think about yet another lingering and equally important question. If Barack Obama really had been raised in Africa, would he be president of the United States today?

God works in ways never understood by humans. Doesn't He?

Jaytoe Anthony Tukan, Sr.

Citizenship or Birthright

Natural-born citizen

"Who is a natural-born citizen? Who, in other words, is a citizen at birth, such that that person can be a President someday?"

INA: ACT 301-
NATIONALS AND CITIZENS OF THE UNITED STATES AT BIRTH

Sec. 301. {8 U.S.C. 1401} (g) "A person born outside the geographical limits of the United States and its outlying possessions of parents one of whom is an alien, and the other a citizen of the United States, who, prior to the birth of such person, was physically present in the United States or its outlying possessions for a period not less than five years, at

Jaytoe Anthony Tukan, Sr.

least two of which were after attaining the age of fourteen years."

While the author still believes that Barack Obama was born in Haiwai, and is therefore a citizen of the United States, the above amendment to the United States Constitution was necessary to be placed in this book, because the President's Citizenship or Birthright has been one of controversy by individuals who still do not see the **handwriting on the wall**. It is the **handwriting of change and healing** that has come to America, but there are others who are still living in the past.

So, my dear reader, there you have it. Even if you still believe that Barack was born in Jakarta, Indonesia, or Nairobi, Kenya, he is still a citizen of the United States, according to the above. Therefore, he is eligible to be president of the United States of America.

For more information on this issue, please read the Fourteenth Amendment to the United States Constitution.

Bibliography

"I am not the candidate of the women's movement of this country, although I am a woman, and I am equally proud of that....." Shirley Chisholm. Retrieved from: www.essortment.com. Rosa Parks, *(Quiet Strength, Zondervan Publishing House, 1994).*

"I've been to the mountaintop..." (Say It Plain, The New Press, 2005), by Katherine Ellis & Stephen Drury Smith.

Author's note: Probably, this was Dr. King's last speech before his assassination.

"I have a dream." (the DREAM, HarperCollins Publisher, 2003), by Drew D. Hansen,

Barack Obama, (Dreams from My Father, Three Rivers Press, New York, NY 1995, 2004).

Sidney Poitier, (The Measure of a Man, Harper -

Collins Publishers, Inc., New York, NY, 2000).

Pictorial History of Black America, Volume Three (The Editors of Ebony Magazine, Johnson Publishing, Inc., Chicago, IL,1971, 1974).
Doris E. Saunders, (Special Moments In African-American History, Johnson Publishing Company, Chicago, IL, 1955-1996, 1998,).

"Man is born free, and everywhere he is in bound chains," Jean-Jacques Rousseau, (Oxford Dictionary of Quotations, page 549, 1941).

The Chicago Tribune (www.chicagotribune.com)

The Baltimore Sun (www.baltimoresun.com)

African Kingdoms of Slavery/Central Africa: 1600 - 1800 A.D. Retrieved from:
www.metmuseum.org.

The Constitution and Its Amendments (Macmilan Reference USA, 1999).

Amendment XIV: Citizenship for All (Greenhaven Press, 2009)

"Democracy is necessary, because man is a brute, and if given his own way, he will use his brutality against his fellow men." Liberian History (Allen Jerome Yancy.......).

All Obama family photographs used in this book are by the courtesy: www.whitehouse.gov and www.barackobama.com

TURNING OF THE TIDE

All other photographs are by the courtesy of Time Life Pictures (www.time.com).

Jaytoe Anthony Tukan, Sr.

TURNING OF THE TIDE

Other books written by the author:

FRIENDSHIPS (The Talk)
Kitty Cat Had A Dream
Little Bernice Animal Book
The Other End Of The Tunnel

Jaytoe Anthony Tukan, Sr.

TURNING OF THE TIDE

Kalawantis Publishing Services, Inc.
Copyright © 2017
Jaytoe Anthony Tukan, Sr.
author@kalawantis.com
publisher@kalawantis.com
www.kalawantis.com

Jaytoe Anthony Tukan, Sr.

www.ingramcontent.com/pod-product-compliance
Lightning Source LLC
Chambersburg PA
CBHW030439290526
45786CB00001B/352